C-2001   CAREER EXAMINATION SERIES

This is your
PASSBOOK® for...

Town Engineer

Test Preparation Study Guide
Questions & Answers

NATIONAL LEARNING CORPORATION®

COPYRIGHT NOTICE

This book is SOLELY intended for, is sold ONLY to, and its use is RESTRICTED to individual, bona fide applicants or candidates who qualify by virtue of having seriously filed applications for appropriate license, certificate, professional and/or promotional advancement, higher school matriculation, scholarship, or other legitimate requirements of education and/or governmental authorities.

This book is NOT intended for use, class instruction, tutoring, training, duplication, copying, reprinting, excerption, or adaptation, etc., by:

1) Other publishers
2) Proprietors and/or Instructors of "Coaching" and/or Preparatory Courses
3) Personnel and/or Training Divisions of commercial, industrial, and governmental organizations
4) Schools, colleges, or universities and/or their departments and staffs, including teachers and other personnel
5) Testing Agencies or Bureaus
6) Study groups which seek by the purchase of a single volume to copy and/or duplicate and/or adapt this material for use by the group as a whole without having purchased individual volumes for each of the members of the group
7) Et al.

Such persons would be in violation of appropriate Federal and State statutes.

PROVISION OF LICENSING AGREEMENTS – Recognized educational, commercial, industrial, and governmental institutions and organizations, and others legitimately engaged in educational pursuits, including training, testing, and measurement activities, may address request for a licensing agreement to the copyright owners, who will determine whether, and under what conditions, including fees and charges, the materials in this book may be used them. In other words, a licensing facility exists for the legitimate use of the material in this book on other than an individual basis. However, it is asseverated and affirmed here that the material in this book CANNOT be used without the receipt of the express permission of such a licensing agreement from the Publishers. Inquiries re licensing should be addressed to the company, attention rights and permissions department.

All rights reserved, including the right of reproduction in whole or in part, in any form or by any means, electronic or mechanical, including photocopying, recording, or by any information storage and retrieval system, without permission in writing from the Publisher.

Copyright © 2025 by
National Learning Corporation

212 Michael Drive, Syosset, NY 11791
(516) 921-8888 • www.passbooks.com
E-mail: info@passbooks.com

PASSBOOK® SERIES

THE *PASSBOOK® SERIES* has been created to prepare applicants and candidates for the ultimate academic battlefield – the examination room.

At some time in our lives, each and every one of us may be required to take an examination – for validation, matriculation, admission, qualification, registration, certification, or licensure.

Based on the assumption that every applicant or candidate has met the basic formal educational standards, has taken the required number of courses, and read the necessary texts, the *PASSBOOK® SERIES* furnishes the one special preparation which may assure passing with confidence, instead of failing with insecurity. Examination questions – together with answers – are furnished as the basic vehicle for study so that the mysteries of the examination and its compounding difficulties may be eliminated or diminished by a sure method.

This book is meant to help you pass your examination provided that you qualify and are serious in your objective.

The entire field is reviewed through the huge store of content information which is succinctly presented through a provocative and challenging approach – the question-and-answer method.

A climate of success is established by furnishing the correct answers at the end of each test.

You soon learn to recognize types of questions, forms of questions, and patterns of questioning. You may even begin to anticipate expected outcomes.

You perceive that many questions are repeated or adapted so that you can gain acute insights, which may enable you to score many sure points.

You learn how to confront new questions, or types of questions, and to attack them confidently and work out the correct answers.

You note objectives and emphases, and recognize pitfalls and dangers, so that you may make positive educational adjustments.

Moreover, you are kept fully informed in relation to new concepts, methods, practices, and directions in the field.

You discover that you are actually taking the examination all the time: you are preparing for the examination by "taking" an examination, not by reading extraneous and/or supererogatory textbooks.

In short, this PASSBOOK®, used directedly, should be an important factor in helping you to pass your test.

TOWN ENGINEER

DUTIES
An employee in this class is responsible for planning, organizing and directing all engineering functions of a building and planning department. Performs professional engineering and administrative work in the development and maintenance of town facilities. The principal responsibilities are for determining and establishing technical and administrative policies, and procedures for the development, analysis and evaluation of engineering projects with respect to their feasibility, cost, economic justification and public necessity and convenience. Supervision is exercised directly or indirectly over all departmental employees. Does related work as required.

SCOPE OF THE EXAMINATION
The written test will cover knowledge, skills and/or abilities in such areas as:

1. Principles and practices of civil engineering;
2. Construction and maintenance of highways, bridges, drainage systems and other related structures;
3. Building construction principles, practices and materials;
4. Building, housing and zoning laws and codes;
5. Engineering estimates and specifications;
6. Principles of project management, including contracts, contract administration and construction economics;
7. Administrative supervision; and
8. Preparing written material.

HOW TO TAKE A TEST

I. YOU MUST PASS AN EXAMINATION

A. *WHAT EVERY CANDIDATE SHOULD KNOW*

Examination applicants often ask us for help in preparing for the written test. What can I study in advance? What kinds of questions will be asked? How will the test be given? How will the papers be graded?

As an applicant for a civil service examination, you may be wondering about some of these things. Our purpose here is to suggest effective methods of advance study and to describe civil service examinations.

Your chances for success on this examination can be increased if you know how to prepare. Those "pre-examination jitters" can be reduced if you know what to expect. You can even experience an adventure in good citizenship if you know why civil service exams are given.

B. *WHY ARE CIVIL SERVICE EXAMINATIONS GIVEN?*

Civil service examinations are important to you in two ways. As a citizen, you want public jobs filled by employees who know how to do their work. As a job seeker, you want a fair chance to compete for that job on an equal footing with other candidates. The best-known means of accomplishing this two-fold goal is the competitive examination.

Exams are widely publicized throughout the nation. They may be administered for jobs in federal, state, city, municipal, town or village governments or agencies.

Any citizen may apply, with some limitations, such as the age or residence of applicants. Your experience and education may be reviewed to see whether you meet the requirements for the particular examination. When these requirements exist, they are reasonable and applied consistently to all applicants. Thus, a competitive examination may cause you some uneasiness now, but it is your privilege and safeguard.

C. *HOW ARE CIVIL SERVICE EXAMS DEVELOPED?*

Examinations are carefully written by trained technicians who are specialists in the field known as "psychological measurement," in consultation with recognized authorities in the field of work that the test will cover. These experts recommend the subject matter areas or skills to be tested; only those knowledges or skills important to your success on the job are included. The most reliable books and source materials available are used as references. Together, the experts and technicians judge the difficulty level of the questions.

Test technicians know how to phrase questions so that the problem is clearly stated. Their ethics do not permit "trick" or "catch" questions. Questions may have been tried out on sample groups, or subjected to statistical analysis, to determine their usefulness.

Written tests are often used in combination with performance tests, ratings of training and experience, and oral interviews. All of these measures combine to form the best-known means of finding the right person for the right job.

II. HOW TO PASS THE WRITTEN TEST

A. NATURE OF THE EXAMINATION

To prepare intelligently for civil service examinations, you should know how they differ from school examinations you have taken. In school you were assigned certain definite pages to read or subjects to cover. The examination questions were quite detailed and usually emphasized memory. Civil service exams, on the other hand, try to discover your present ability to perform the duties of a position, plus your potentiality to learn these duties. In other words, a civil service exam attempts to predict how successful you will be. Questions cover such a broad area that they cannot be as minute and detailed as school exam questions.

In the public service similar kinds of work, or positions, are grouped together in one "class." This process is known as *position-classification*. All the positions in a class are paid according to the salary range for that class. One class title covers all of these positions, and they are all tested by the same examination.

B. FOUR BASIC STEPS

1) Study the announcement

How, then, can you know what subjects to study? Our best answer is: "Learn as much as possible about the class of positions for which you've applied." The exam will test the knowledge, skills and abilities needed to do the work.

Your most valuable source of information about the position you want is the official exam announcement. This announcement lists the training and experience qualifications. Check these standards and apply only if you come reasonably close to meeting them.

The brief description of the position in the examination announcement offers some clues to the subjects which will be tested. Think about the job itself. Review the duties in your mind. Can you perform them, or are there some in which you are rusty? Fill in the blank spots in your preparation.

Many jurisdictions preview the written test in the exam announcement by including a section called "Knowledge and Abilities Required," "Scope of the Examination," or some similar heading. Here you will find out specifically what fields will be tested.

2) Review your own background

Once you learn in general what the position is all about, and what you need to know to do the work, ask yourself which subjects you already know fairly well and which need improvement. You may wonder whether to concentrate on improving your strong areas or on building some background in your fields of weakness. When the announcement has specified "some knowledge" or "considerable knowledge," or has used adjectives like "beginning principles of…" or "advanced … methods," you can get a clue as to the number and difficulty of questions to be asked in any given field. More questions, and hence broader coverage, would be included for those subjects which are more important in the work. Now weigh your strengths and weaknesses against the job requirements and prepare accordingly.

3) Determine the level of the position

Another way to tell how intensively you should prepare is to understand the level of the job for which you are applying. Is it the entering level? In other words, is this the position in which beginners in a field of work are hired? Or is it an intermediate or advanced level? Sometimes this is indicated by such words as "Junior" or "Senior" in the class title. Other jurisdictions use Roman numerals to designate the level – Clerk I, Clerk II, for example. The word "Supervisor" sometimes appears in the title. If the level is not indicated by the title, check the description of duties. Will you be working under very close supervision, or will you have responsibility for independent decisions in this work?

4) Choose appropriate study materials

Now that you know the subjects to be examined and the relative amount of each subject to be covered, you can choose suitable study materials. For beginning level jobs, or even advanced ones, if you have a pronounced weakness in some aspect of your training, read a modern, standard textbook in that field. Be sure it is up to date and has general coverage. Such books are normally available at your library, and the librarian will be glad to help you locate one. For entry-level positions, questions of appropriate difficulty are chosen – neither highly advanced questions, nor those too simple. Such questions require careful thought but not advanced training.

If the position for which you are applying is technical or advanced, you will read more advanced, specialized material. If you are already familiar with the basic principles of your field, elementary textbooks would waste your time. Concentrate on advanced textbooks and technical periodicals. Think through the concepts and review difficult problems in your field.

These are all general sources. You can get more ideas on your own initiative, following these leads. For example, training manuals and publications of the government agency which employs workers in your field can be useful, particularly for technical and professional positions. A letter or visit to the government department involved may result in more specific study suggestions, and certainly will provide you with a more definite idea of the exact nature of the position you are seeking.

III. KINDS OF TESTS

Tests are used for purposes other than measuring knowledge and ability to perform specified duties. For some positions, it is equally important to test ability to make adjustments to new situations or to profit from training. In others, basic mental abilities not dependent on information are essential. Questions which test these things may not appear as pertinent to the duties of the position as those which test for knowledge and information. Yet they are often highly important parts of a fair examination. For very general questions, it is almost impossible to help you direct your study efforts. What we can do is to point out some of the more common of these general abilities needed in public service positions and describe some typical questions.

1) General information

Broad, general information has been found useful for predicting job success in some kinds of work. This is tested in a variety of ways, from vocabulary lists to questions about current events. Basic background in some field of work, such as sociology or economics, may be sampled in a group of questions. Often these are principles which have become familiar to most persons through exposure rather than through formal training. It is difficult to advise you how to study for these questions; being alert to the world around you is our best suggestion.

2) Verbal ability

An example of an ability needed in many positions is verbal or language ability. Verbal ability is, in brief, the ability to use and understand words. Vocabulary and grammar tests are typical measures of this ability. Reading comprehension or paragraph interpretation questions are common in many kinds of civil service tests. You are given a paragraph of written material and asked to find its central meaning.

3) Numerical ability

Number skills can be tested by the familiar arithmetic problem, by checking paired lists of numbers to see which are alike and which are different, or by interpreting charts and graphs. In the latter test, a graph may be printed in the test booklet which you are asked to use as the basis for answering questions.

4) Observation

A popular test for law-enforcement positions is the observation test. A picture is shown to you for several minutes, then taken away. Questions about the picture test your ability to observe both details and larger elements.

5) Following directions

In many positions in the public service, the employee must be able to carry out written instructions dependably and accurately. You may be given a chart with several columns, each column listing a variety of information. The questions require you to carry out directions involving the information given in the chart.

6) Skills and aptitudes

Performance tests effectively measure some manual skills and aptitudes. When the skill is one in which you are trained, such as typing or shorthand, you can practice. These tests are often very much like those given in business school or high school courses. For many of the other skills and aptitudes, however, no short-time preparation can be made. Skills and abilities natural to you or that you have developed throughout your lifetime are being tested.

Many of the general questions just described provide all the data needed to answer the questions and ask you to use your reasoning ability to find the answers. Your best preparation for these tests, as well as for tests of facts and ideas, is to be at your physical and mental best. You, no doubt, have your own methods of getting into an exam-taking mood and keeping "in shape." The next section lists some ideas on this subject.

IV. KINDS OF QUESTIONS

Only rarely is the "essay" question, which you answer in narrative form, used in civil service tests. Civil service tests are usually of the short-answer type. Full instructions for answering these questions will be given to you at the examination. But in case this is your first experience with short-answer questions and separate answer sheets, here is what you need to know:

1) Multiple-choice Questions

Most popular of the short-answer questions is the "multiple choice" or "best answer" question. It can be used, for example, to test for factual knowledge, ability to solve problems or judgment in meeting situations found at work.

A multiple-choice question is normally one of three types—
- It can begin with an incomplete statement followed by several possible endings. You are to find the one ending which *best* completes the statement, although some of the others may not be entirely wrong.
- It can also be a complete statement in the form of a question which is answered by choosing one of the statements listed.

- It can be in the form of a problem – again you select the best answer.

Here is an example of a multiple-choice question with a discussion which should give you some clues as to the method for choosing the right answer:

When an employee has a complaint about his assignment, the action which will *best* help him overcome his difficulty is to
   A. discuss his difficulty with his coworkers
   B. take the problem to the head of the organization
   C. take the problem to the person who gave him the assignment
   D. say nothing to anyone about his complaint

In answering this question, you should study each of the choices to find which is best. Consider choice "A" – Certainly an employee may discuss his complaint with fellow employees, but no change or improvement can result, and the complaint remains unresolved. Choice "B" is a poor choice since the head of the organization probably does not know what assignment you have been given, and taking your problem to him is known as "going over the head" of the supervisor. The supervisor, or person who made the assignment, is the person who can clarify it or correct any injustice. Choice "C" is, therefore, correct. To say nothing, as in choice "D," is unwise. Supervisors have and interest in knowing the problems employees are facing, and the employee is seeking a solution to his problem.

2) True/False Questions

The "true/false" or "right/wrong" form of question is sometimes used. Here a complete statement is given. Your job is to decide whether the statement is right or wrong.

SAMPLE: A roaming cell-phone call to a nearby city costs less than a non-roaming call to a distant city.

This statement is wrong, or false, since roaming calls are more expensive.

This is not a complete list of all possible question forms, although most of the others are variations of these common types. You will always get complete directions for answering questions. Be sure you understand *how* to mark your answers – ask questions until you do.

V. RECORDING YOUR ANSWERS

Computer terminals are used more and more today for many different kinds of exams.
For an examination with very few applicants, you may be told to record your answers in the test booklet itself. Separate answer sheets are much more common. If this separate answer sheet is to be scored by machine – and this is often the case – it is highly important that you mark your answers correctly in order to get credit.

An electronic scoring machine is often used in civil service offices because of the speed with which papers can be scored. Machine-scored answer sheets must be marked with a pencil, which will be given to you. This pencil has a high graphite content which responds to the electronic scoring machine. As a matter of fact, stray dots may register as answers, so do not let your pencil rest on the answer sheet while you are pondering the correct answer. Also, if your pencil lead breaks or is otherwise defective, ask for another.

Since the answer sheet will be dropped in a slot in the scoring machine, be careful not to bend the corners or get the paper crumpled.

The answer sheet normally has five vertical columns of numbers, with 30 numbers to a column. These numbers correspond to the question numbers in your test booklet. After each number, going across the page are four or five pairs of dotted lines. These short dotted lines have small letters or numbers above them. The first two pairs may also have a "T" or "F" above the letters. This indicates that the first two pairs only are to be used if the questions are of the true-false type. If the questions are multiple choice, disregard the "T" and "F" and pay attention only to the small letters or numbers.

Answer your questions in the manner of the sample that follows:

32. The largest city in the United States is
   A. Washington, D.C.
   B. New York City
   C. Chicago
   D. Detroit
   E. San Francisco

1) Choose the answer you think is best. (New York City is the largest, so "B" is correct.)
2) Find the row of dotted lines numbered the same as the question you are answering. (Find row number 32)
3) Find the pair of dotted lines corresponding to the answer. (Find the pair of lines under the mark "B.")
4) Make a solid black mark between the dotted lines.

VI. BEFORE THE TEST

Common sense will help you find procedures to follow to get ready for an examination. Too many of us, however, overlook these sensible measures. Indeed, nervousness and fatigue have been found to be the most serious reasons why applicants fail to do their best on civil service tests. Here is a list of reminders:

- Begin your preparation early – Don't wait until the last minute to go scurrying around for books and materials or to find out what the position is all about.
- Prepare continuously – An hour a night for a week is better than an all-night cram session. This has been definitely established. What is more, a night a week for a month will return better dividends than crowding your study into a shorter period of time.
- Locate the place of the exam – You have been sent a notice telling you when and where to report for the examination. If the location is in a different town or otherwise unfamiliar to you, it would be well to inquire the best route and learn something about the building.
- Relax the night before the test – Allow your mind to rest. Do not study at all that night. Plan some mild recreation or diversion; then go to bed early and get a good night's sleep.
- Get up early enough to make a leisurely trip to the place for the test – This way unforeseen events, traffic snarls, unfamiliar buildings, etc. will not upset you.
- Dress comfortably – A written test is not a fashion show. You will be known by number and not by name, so wear something comfortable.

- Leave excess paraphernalia at home – Shopping bags and odd bundles will get in your way. You need bring only the items mentioned in the official notice you received; usually everything you need is provided. Do not bring reference books to the exam. They will only confuse those last minutes and be taken away from you when in the test room.
- Arrive somewhat ahead of time – If because of transportation schedules you must get there very early, bring a newspaper or magazine to take your mind off yourself while waiting.
- Locate the examination room – When you have found the proper room, you will be directed to the seat or part of the room where you will sit. Sometimes you are given a sheet of instructions to read while you are waiting. Do not fill out any forms until you are told to do so; just read them and be prepared.
- Relax and prepare to listen to the instructions
- If you have any physical problem that may keep you from doing your best, be sure to tell the test administrator. If you are sick or in poor health, you really cannot do your best on the exam. You can come back and take the test some other time.

VII. AT THE TEST

The day of the test is here and you have the test booklet in your hand. The temptation to get going is very strong. Caution! There is more to success than knowing the right answers. You must know how to identify your papers and understand variations in the type of short-answer question used in this particular examination. Follow these suggestions for maximum results from your efforts:

1) Cooperate with the monitor

The test administrator has a duty to create a situation in which you can be as much at ease as possible. He will give instructions, tell you when to begin, check to see that you are marking your answer sheet correctly, and so on. He is not there to guard you, although he will see that your competitors do not take unfair advantage. He wants to help you do your best.

2) Listen to all instructions

Don't jump the gun! Wait until you understand all directions. In most civil service tests you get more time than you need to answer the questions. So don't be in a hurry. Read each word of instructions until you clearly understand the meaning. Study the examples, listen to all announcements and follow directions. Ask questions if you do not understand what to do.

3) Identify your papers

Civil service exams are usually identified by number only. You will be assigned a number; you must not put your name on your test papers. Be sure to copy your number correctly. Since more than one exam may be given, copy your exact examination title.

4) Plan your time

Unless you are told that a test is a "speed" or "rate of work" test, speed itself is usually not important. Time enough to answer all the questions will be provided, but this does not mean that you have all day. An overall time limit has been set. Divide the total time (in minutes) by the number of questions to determine the approximate time you have for each question.

5) Do not linger over difficult questions

If you come across a difficult question, mark it with a paper clip (useful to have along) and come back to it when you have been through the booklet. One caution if you do this – be sure to skip a number on your answer sheet as well. Check often to be sure that you have not lost your place and that you are marking in the row numbered the same as the question you are answering.

6) Read the questions

Be sure you know what the question asks! Many capable people are unsuccessful because they failed to *read* the questions correctly.

7) Answer all questions

Unless you have been instructed that a penalty will be deducted for incorrect answers, it is better to guess than to omit a question.

8) Speed tests

It is often better NOT to guess on speed tests. It has been found that on timed tests people are tempted to spend the last few seconds before time is called in marking answers at random – without even reading them – in the hope of picking up a few extra points. To discourage this practice, the instructions may warn you that your score will be "corrected" for guessing. That is, a penalty will be applied. The incorrect answers will be deducted from the correct ones, or some other penalty formula will be used.

9) Review your answers

If you finish before time is called, go back to the questions you guessed or omitted to give them further thought. Review other answers if you have time.

10) Return your test materials

If you are ready to leave before others have finished or time is called, take ALL your materials to the monitor and leave quietly. Never take any test material with you. The monitor can discover whose papers are not complete, and taking a test booklet may be grounds for disqualification.

VIII. EXAMINATION TECHNIQUES

1) Read the general instructions carefully. These are usually printed on the first page of the exam booklet. As a rule, these instructions refer to the timing of the examination; the fact that you should not start work until the signal and must stop work at a signal, etc. If there are any *special* instructions, such as a choice of questions to be answered, make sure that you note this instruction carefully.

2) When you are ready to start work on the examination, that is as soon as the signal has been given, read the instructions to each question booklet, underline any key words or phrases, such as *least, best, outline, describe* and the like. In this way you will tend to answer as requested rather than discover on reviewing your paper that you *listed without describing*, that you selected the *worst* choice rather than the *best* choice, etc.

3) If the examination is of the objective or multiple-choice type – that is, each question will also give a series of possible answers: A, B, C or D, and you are called upon to select the best answer and write the letter next to that answer on your answer paper – it is advisable to start answering each question in turn. There may be anywhere from 50 to 100 such questions in the three or four hours allotted and you can see how much time would be taken if you read through all the questions before beginning to answer any. Furthermore, if you come across a question or group of questions which you know would be difficult to answer, it would undoubtedly affect your handling of all the other questions.

4) If the examination is of the essay type and contains but a few questions, it is a moot point as to whether you should read all the questions before starting to answer any one. Of course, if you are given a choice – say five out of seven and the like – then it is essential to read all the questions so you can eliminate the two that are most difficult. If, however, you are asked to answer all the questions, there may be danger in trying to answer the easiest one first because you may find that you will spend too much time on it. The best technique is to answer the first question, then proceed to the second, etc.

5) Time your answers. Before the exam begins, write down the time it started, then add the time allowed for the examination and write down the time it must be completed, then divide the time available somewhat as follows:
    - If 3-1/2 hours are allowed, that would be 210 minutes. If you have 80 objective-type questions, that would be an average of 2-1/2 minutes per question. Allow yourself no more than 2 minutes per question, or a total of 160 minutes, which will permit about 50 minutes to review.
    - If for the time allotment of 210 minutes there are 7 essay questions to answer, that would average about 30 minutes a question. Give yourself only 25 minutes per question so that you have about 35 minutes to review.

6) The most important instruction is to *read each question* and make sure you know what is wanted. The second most important instruction is to *time yourself properly* so that you answer every question. The third most important instruction is to *answer every question*. Guess if you have to but include something for each question. Remember that you will receive no credit for a blank and will probably receive some credit if you write something in answer to an essay question. If you guess a letter – say "B" for a multiple-choice question – you may have guessed right. If you leave a blank as an answer to a multiple-choice question, the examiners may respect your feelings but it will not add a point to your score. Some exams may penalize you for wrong answers, so in such cases *only*, you may not want to guess unless you have some basis for your answer.

7) Suggestions
    a. Objective-type questions
        1. Examine the question booklet for proper sequence of pages and questions
        2. Read all instructions carefully
        3. Skip any question which seems too difficult; return to it after all other questions have been answered
        4. Apportion your time properly; do not spend too much time on any single question or group of questions

5. Note and underline key words – *all, most, fewest, least, best, worst, same, opposite,* etc.
6. Pay particular attention to negatives
7. Note unusual option, e.g., unduly long, short, complex, different or similar in content to the body of the question
8. Observe the use of "hedging" words – *probably, may, most likely,* etc.
9. Make sure that your answer is put next to the same number as the question
10. Do not second-guess unless you have good reason to believe the second answer is definitely more correct
11. Cross out original answer if you decide another answer is more accurate; do not erase until you are ready to hand your paper in
12. Answer all questions; guess unless instructed otherwise
13. Leave time for review

  b. Essay questions
1. Read each question carefully
2. Determine exactly what is wanted. Underline key words or phrases.
3. Decide on outline or paragraph answer
4. Include many different points and elements unless asked to develop any one or two points or elements
5. Show impartiality by giving pros and cons unless directed to select one side only
6. Make and write down any assumptions you find necessary to answer the questions
7. Watch your English, grammar, punctuation and choice of words
8. Time your answers; don't crowd material

8) Answering the essay question

Most essay questions can be answered by framing the specific response around several key words or ideas. Here are a few such key words or ideas:

M's: manpower, materials, methods, money, management
P's: purpose, program, policy, plan, procedure, practice, problems, pitfalls, personnel, public relations

  a. Six basic steps in handling problems:
1. Preliminary plan and background development
2. Collect information, data and facts
3. Analyze and interpret information, data and facts
4. Analyze and develop solutions as well as make recommendations
5. Prepare report and sell recommendations
6. Install recommendations and follow up effectiveness

  b. Pitfalls to avoid
1. *Taking things for granted* – A statement of the situation does not necessarily imply that each of the elements is necessarily true; for example, a complaint may be invalid and biased so that all that can be taken for granted is that a complaint has been registered

2. *Considering only one side of a situation* – Wherever possible, indicate several alternatives and then point out the reasons you selected the best one
3. *Failing to indicate follow up* – Whenever your answer indicates action on your part, make certain that you will take proper follow-up action to see how successful your recommendations, procedures or actions turn out to be
4. *Taking too long in answering any single question* – Remember to time your answers properly

IX. AFTER THE TEST

Scoring procedures differ in detail among civil service jurisdictions although the general principles are the same. Whether the papers are hand-scored or graded by machine we have described, they are nearly always graded by number. That is, the person who marks the paper knows only the number – never the name – of the applicant. Not until all the papers have been graded will they be matched with names. If other tests, such as training and experience or oral interview ratings have been given, scores will be combined. Different parts of the examination usually have different weights. For example, the written test might count 60 percent of the final grade, and a rating of training and experience 40 percent. In many jurisdictions, veterans will have a certain number of points added to their grades.

After the final grade has been determined, the names are placed in grade order and an eligible list is established. There are various methods for resolving ties between those who get the same final grade – probably the most common is to place first the name of the person whose application was received first. Job offers are made from the eligible list in the order the names appear on it. You will be notified of your grade and your rank as soon as all these computations have been made. This will be done as rapidly as possible.

People who are found to meet the requirements in the announcement are called "eligibles." Their names are put on a list of eligible candidates. An eligible's chances of getting a job depend on how high he stands on this list and how fast agencies are filling jobs from the list.

When a job is to be filled from a list of eligibles, the agency asks for the names of people on the list of eligibles for that job. When the civil service commission receives this request, it sends to the agency the names of the three people highest on this list. Or, if the job to be filled has specialized requirements, the office sends the agency the names of the top three persons who meet these requirements from the general list.

The appointing officer makes a choice from among the three people whose names were sent to him. If the selected person accepts the appointment, the names of the others are put back on the list to be considered for future openings.

That is the rule in hiring from all kinds of eligible lists, whether they are for typist, carpenter, chemist, or something else. For every vacancy, the appointing officer has his choice of any one of the top three eligibles on the list. This explains why the person whose name is on top of the list sometimes does not get an appointment when some of the persons lower on the list do. If the appointing officer chooses the second or third eligible, the No. 1 eligible does not get a job at once, but stays on the list until he is appointed or the list is terminated.

X. HOW TO PASS THE INTERVIEW TEST

The examination for which you applied requires an oral interview test. You have already taken the written test and you are now being called for the interview test – the final part of the formal examination.

You may think that it is not possible to prepare for an interview test and that there are no procedures to follow during an interview. Our purpose is to point out some things you can do in advance that will help you and some good rules to follow and pitfalls to avoid while you are being interviewed.

What is an interview supposed to test?

The written examination is designed to test the technical knowledge and competence of the candidate; the oral is designed to evaluate intangible qualities, not readily measured otherwise, and to establish a list showing the relative fitness of each candidate – as measured against his competitors – for the position sought. Scoring is not on the basis of "right" and "wrong," but on a sliding scale of values ranging from "not passable" to "outstanding." As a matter of fact, it is possible to achieve a relatively low score without a single "incorrect" answer because of evident weakness in the qualities being measured.

Occasionally, an examination may consist entirely of an oral test – either an individual or a group oral. In such cases, information is sought concerning the technical knowledges and abilities of the candidate, since there has been no written examination for this purpose. More commonly, however, an oral test is used to supplement a written examination.

Who conducts interviews?

The composition of oral boards varies among different jurisdictions. In nearly all, a representative of the personnel department serves as chairman. One of the members of the board may be a representative of the department in which the candidate would work. In some cases, "outside experts" are used, and, frequently, a businessman or some other representative of the general public is asked to serve. Labor and management or other special groups may be represented. The aim is to secure the services of experts in the appropriate field.

However the board is composed, it is a good idea (and not at all improper or unethical) to ascertain in advance of the interview who the members are and what groups they represent. When you are introduced to them, you will have some idea of their backgrounds and interests, and at least you will not stutter and stammer over their names.

What should be done before the interview?

While knowledge about the board members is useful and takes some of the surprise element out of the interview, there is other preparation which is more substantive. It *is* possible to prepare for an oral interview – in several ways:

1) Keep a copy of your application and review it carefully before the interview

This may be the only document before the oral board, and the starting point of the interview. Know what education and experience you have listed there, and the sequence and dates of all of it. Sometimes the board will ask you to review the highlights of your experience for them; you should not have to hem and haw doing it.

2) Study the class specification and the examination announcement

Usually, the oral board has one or both of these to guide them. The qualities, characteristics or knowledges required by the position sought are stated in these documents. They offer valuable clues as to the nature of the oral interview. For example, if the job involves supervisory responsibilities, the announcement will usually indicate that knowledge of modern supervisory methods and the qualifications of the candidate as a supervisor will be tested. If so, you can expect such questions, frequently in the form of a hypothetical situation which you are expected to solve. NEVER go into an oral without knowledge of the duties and responsibilities of the job you seek.

3) Think through each qualification required

Try to visualize the kind of questions you would ask if you were a board member. How well could you answer them? Try especially to appraise your own knowledge and background in each area, *measured against the job sought*, and identify any areas in which you are weak. Be critical and realistic – do not flatter yourself.

4) Do some general reading in areas in which you feel you may be weak

For example, if the job involves supervision and your past experience has NOT, some general reading in supervisory methods and practices, particularly in the field of human relations, might be useful. Do NOT study agency procedures or detailed manuals. The oral board will be testing your understanding and capacity, not your memory.

5) Get a good night's sleep and watch your general health and mental attitude

You will want a clear head at the interview. Take care of a cold or any other minor ailment, and of course, no hangovers.

What should be done on the day of the interview?

Now comes the day of the interview itself. Give yourself plenty of time to get there. Plan to arrive somewhat ahead of the scheduled time, particularly if your appointment is in the fore part of the day. If a previous candidate fails to appear, the board might be ready for you a bit early. By early afternoon an oral board is almost invariably behind schedule if there are many candidates, and you may have to wait. Take along a book or magazine to read, or your application to review, but leave any extraneous material in the waiting room when you go in for your interview. In any event, relax and compose yourself.

The matter of dress is important. The board is forming impressions about you – from your experience, your manners, your attitude, and your appearance. Give your personal appearance careful attention. Dress your best, but not your flashiest. Choose conservative, appropriate clothing, and be sure it is immaculate. This is a business interview, and your appearance should indicate that you regard it as such. Besides, being well groomed and properly dressed will help boost your confidence.

Sooner or later, someone will call your name and escort you into the interview room. *This is it.* From here on you are on your own. It is too late for any more preparation. But remember, you asked for this opportunity to prove your fitness, and you are here because your request was granted.

What happens when you go in?

The usual sequence of events will be as follows: The clerk (who is often the board stenographer) will introduce you to the chairman of the oral board, who will introduce you to the other members of the board. Acknowledge the introductions before you sit down. Do not be surprised if you find a microphone facing you or a stenotypist sitting by. Oral interviews are usually recorded in the event of an appeal or other review.

Usually the chairman of the board will open the interview by reviewing the highlights of your education and work experience from your application – primarily for the benefit of the other members of the board, as well as to get the material into the record. Do not interrupt or comment unless there is an error or significant misinterpretation; if that is the case, do not hesitate. But do not quibble about insignificant matters. Also, he will usually ask you some question about your education, experience or your present job – partly to get you to start talking and to establish the interviewing "rapport." He may start the actual questioning, or turn it over to one of the other members. Frequently, each member undertakes the questioning on a particular area, one in which he is perhaps most competent, so you can expect each member to participate in the examination. Because time is limited, you may also expect some rather abrupt switches in the direction the questioning takes, so do not be upset by it. Normally, a board member will not pursue a single line of questioning unless he discovers a particular strength or weakness.

After each member has participated, the chairman will usually ask whether any member has any further questions, then will ask you if you have anything you wish to add. Unless you are expecting this question, it may floor you. Worse, it may start you off on an extended, extemporaneous speech. The board is not usually seeking more information. The question is principally to offer you a last opportunity to present further qualifications or to indicate that you have nothing to add. So, if you feel that a significant qualification or characteristic has been overlooked, it is proper to point it out in a sentence or so. Do not compliment the board on the thoroughness of their examination – they have been sketchy, and you know it. If you wish, merely say, "No thank you, I have nothing further to add." This is a point where you can "talk yourself out" of a good impression or fail to present an important bit of information. Remember, *you close the interview yourself.*

The chairman will then say, "That is all, Mr. _____, thank you." Do not be startled; the interview is over, and quicker than you think. Thank him, gather your belongings and take your leave. Save your sigh of relief for the other side of the door.

How to put your best foot forward
Throughout this entire process, you may feel that the board individually and collectively is trying to pierce your defenses, seek out your hidden weaknesses and embarrass and confuse you. Actually, this is not true. They are obliged to make an appraisal of your qualifications for the job you are seeking, and they want to see you in your best light. Remember, they must interview all candidates and a non-cooperative candidate may become a failure in spite of their best efforts to bring out his qualifications. Here are 15 suggestions that will help you:

1) Be natural – Keep your attitude confident, not cocky
If you are not confident that you can do the job, do not expect the board to be. Do not apologize for your weaknesses, try to bring out your strong points. The board is interested in a positive, not negative, presentation. Cockiness will antagonize any board member and make him wonder if you are covering up a weakness by a false show of strength.

2) Get comfortable, but don't lounge or sprawl
Sit erectly but not stiffly. A careless posture may lead the board to conclude that you are careless in other things, or at least that you are not impressed by the importance of the occasion. Either conclusion is natural, even if incorrect. Do not fuss with your clothing, a pencil or an ashtray. Your hands may occasionally be useful to emphasize a point; do not let them become a point of distraction.

3) Do not wisecrack or make small talk
This is a serious situation, and your attitude should show that you consider it as such. Further, the time of the board is limited – they do not want to waste it, and neither should you.

4) Do not exaggerate your experience or abilities

In the first place, from information in the application or other interviews and sources, the board may know more about you than you think. Secondly, you probably will not get away with it. An experienced board is rather adept at spotting such a situation, so do not take the chance.

5) If you know a board member, do not make a point of it, yet do not hide it

Certainly you are not fooling him, and probably not the other members of the board. Do not try to take advantage of your acquaintanceship – it will probably do you little good.

6) Do not dominate the interview

Let the board do that. They will give you the clues – do not assume that you have to do all the talking. Realize that the board has a number of questions to ask you, and do not try to take up all the interview time by showing off your extensive knowledge of the answer to the first one.

7) Be attentive

You only have 20 minutes or so, and you should keep your attention at its sharpest throughout. When a member is addressing a problem or question to you, give him your undivided attention. Address your reply principally to him, but do not exclude the other board members.

8) Do not interrupt

A board member may be stating a problem for you to analyze. He will ask you a question when the time comes. Let him state the problem, and wait for the question.

9) Make sure you understand the question

Do not try to answer until you are sure what the question is. If it is not clear, restate it in your own words or ask the board member to clarify it for you. However, do not haggle about minor elements.

10) Reply promptly but not hastily

A common entry on oral board rating sheets is "candidate responded readily," or "candidate hesitated in replies." Respond as promptly and quickly as you can, but do not jump to a hasty, ill-considered answer.

11) Do not be peremptory in your answers

A brief answer is proper – but do not fire your answer back. That is a losing game from your point of view. The board member can probably ask questions much faster than you can answer them.

12) Do not try to create the answer you think the board member wants

He is interested in what kind of mind you have and how it works – not in playing games. Furthermore, he can usually spot this practice and will actually grade you down on it.

13) Do not switch sides in your reply merely to agree with a board member

Frequently, a member will take a contrary position merely to draw you out and to see if you are willing and able to defend your point of view. Do not start a debate, yet do not surrender a good position. If a position is worth taking, it is worth defending.

14) Do not be afraid to admit an error in judgment if you are shown to be wrong

The board knows that you are forced to reply without any opportunity for careful consideration. Your answer may be demonstrably wrong. If so, admit it and get on with the interview.

15) Do not dwell at length on your present job

The opening question may relate to your present assignment. Answer the question but do not go into an extended discussion. You are being examined for a *new* job, not your present one. As a matter of fact, try to phrase ALL your answers in terms of the job for which you are being examined.

Basis of Rating

Probably you will forget most of these "do's" and "don'ts" when you walk into the oral interview room. Even remembering them all will not ensure you a passing grade. Perhaps you did not have the qualifications in the first place. But remembering them will help you to put your best foot forward, without treading on the toes of the board members.

Rumor and popular opinion to the contrary notwithstanding, an oral board wants you to make the best appearance possible. They know you are under pressure – but they also want to see how you respond to it as a guide to what your reaction would be under the pressures of the job you seek. They will be influenced by the degree of poise you display, the personal traits you show and the manner in which you respond.

ABOUT THIS BOOK

This book contains tests divided into Examination Sections. Go through each test, answering every question in the margin. We have also attached a sample answer sheet at the back of the book that can be removed and used. At the end of each test look at the answer key and check your answers. On the ones you got wrong, look at the right answer choice and learn. Do not fill in the answers first. Do not memorize the questions and answers, but understand the answer and principles involved. On your test, the questions will likely be different from the samples. Questions are changed and new ones added. If you understand these past questions you should have success with any changes that arise. Tests may consist of several types of questions. We have additional books on each subject should more study be advisable or necessary for you. Finally, the more you study, the better prepared you will be. This book is intended to be the last thing you study before you walk into the examination room. Prior study of relevant texts is also recommended. NLC publishes some of these in our Fundamental Series. Knowledge and good sense are important factors in passing your exam. Good luck also helps. So now study this Passbook, absorb the material contained within and take that knowledge into the examination. Then do your best to pass that exam.

EXAMINATION SECTION

EXAMINATION SECTION
TEST 1

DIRECTIONS: Each question or incomplete statement is followed by several suggested answers or completions. Select the one that BEST answers the question or completes the statement. *PRINT THE LETTER OF THE CORRECT ANSWER IN THE SPACE AT THE RIGHT.*

1. Management by exception (MBE) is   1.____

    A. designed to locate bottlenecks
    B. designed to pinpoint superior performance
    C. a form of index locating
    D. a form of variance reporting

2. In managerial terms, gap analysis is useful primarily in   2.____

    A. problem solving   B. setting standards
    C. inventory control   D. locating bottlenecks

3. ABC analysis involves   3.____

    A. problem solving   B. indexing
    C. brainstorming   D. inventory control

4. The Federal Discrimination in Employment Act as amended in 1978 prohibits job discrimination based on age for persons between the ages of   4.____

    A. 35 and 60   B. 40 and 65   C. 45 and 65   D. 40 and 70

5. Inspectors should be familiar with the contractor's CPM charts for a construction job primarily to determine if   5.____

    A. the job is on schedule
    B. the contractor is using the charts correctly
    C. material is on hand to keep the job on schedule
    D. there is a potential source of delay

6. The value engineering approach is frequently found in public works contracts. Value engineering is   6.____

    A. an effort to cut down or eliminate extra work payments
    B. a team approach to optimize the cost of the project
    C. to insure that material and equipment will perform as specified
    D. to insure that insurance costs on the project can be minimized

7. Historically, most costly claims have been either for   7.____

    A. unreasonable inspection requirements or unforeseen weather conditions
    B. unreasonable specification requirements or unreasonable completion time for the contract
    C. added costs due to inflation or unavailability of material
    D. delays or alleged changed conditions

1

8. A claim is a

   A. dispute that cannot be resolved
   B. dispute arising from ambiguity in the specifications
   C. dispute arising from the quality of the work
   D. recognition that the courts are the sole arbiters of a dispute

8.___

9. Disputes arising between a contractor and the owning agency are

   A. the result of inflexibility of either or both parties to the dispute
   B. mainly the result of shortcomings in the design
   C. the result of shortcomings in the specifications
   D. inevitable

9.___

Questions 10-13.

DIRECTIONS: Questions 10 through 13, inclusive, refers to the array of numbers listed below.

16, 7, 9, 5, 10, 8, 5, 1, 2

10. The mean of the numbers is

    A. 2   B. 5   C. 7   D. 8

10.___

11. The median of the numbers is

    A. 2   B. 5   C. 7   D. 8

11.___

12. The mode of the numbers is

    A. 2   B. 5   C. 7   D. 8

12.___

13. In statistical measurements, a subgroup that is representative of the entire group is a

    A. commutative group   B. sample
    C. central index   D. Abelian group

13.___

14. Productivity is the ratio of

    A. $\dfrac{\text{product costs}}{\text{labor costs}}$

    B. $\dfrac{\text{cost of final product}}{\text{cost of materials}}$

    C. $\dfrac{\text{outputs}}{\text{inputs}}$

    D. $\dfrac{\text{outputs cost}}{\text{time needed to product the output}}$

14.___

15. Downtime is the time a piece of equipment is

    A. idle waiting for other equipment to become available
    B. not being used for the purpose it was intended

15.___

C. being used inefficiently
D. unavailable for use

16. Index numbers

    A. relates to the cost of a product as material costs vary
    B. allows the user to find the variation from the norm
    C. are a way of comparing costs of different approaches to a problem
    D. a way of measuring and comparing changes over a period of time

16.____

17. The underlying idea behind Management by Objectives is to provide a mechanism for managers to

    A. coordinate personal and departmental plans with organizational goals
    B. motivate employees by having them participate in job decisions
    C. motivate employees by training them for the next higher position
    D. set objectives that are reasonable for the employees to attain, thus improving self-esteem among the employees

17.____

18. The ultimate objective of the project manager in planning and scheduling a project is to

    A. meet the completion dates of the project
    B. use the least amount of labor on the project
    C. use the least amount of material on the project
    D. prevent interference between the different trades

18.____

19. Scheduling with respect to the critical path method usually does not involve

    A. cost allocation
    B. starting and finishing time
    C. float for each activity
    D. project duration

19.____

20. When CPM is used on a construction project, updates are most commonly made

    A. weekly   B. every two weeks
    C. monthly   D. every two months

20.____

Questions 21-24.

DIRECTIONS: Questions 21 through 24 refer to the following network.

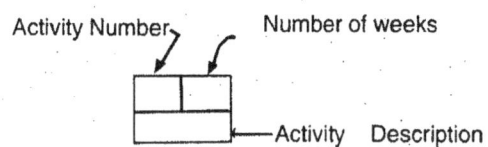

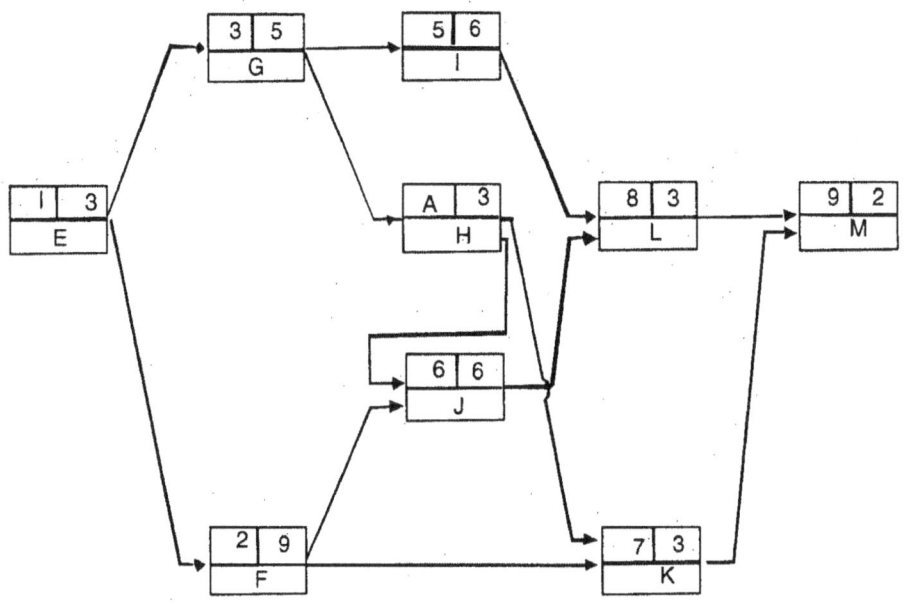

Activity Number	Activity Description	Duration in Weeks	Early Start	Early Finish	Late Start	Late Finish	Total Slack
1	E	3					
2	F	9					
3	G	5					
4	H	3					
5	I	6					
6	J	6					
7	K	3					
8	L	3					
9	M	2					

21. The critical path is

    A. E G H J L M   B. E G I L M
    C. E F J L M   D. E G H K M

21.____

22. The minimum time needed to complete the job is, in weeks,

    A. 19   B. 21   C. 22   D. 23

22.____

23. The slack time in J is, in weeks,

    A. 0   B. 1   C. 2   D. 3

23.____

24. The slack time in K is, in weeks,

    A. 4   B. 5   C. 6   D. 7

24.____

25. Of the following, the primary objective of CPM is to 25.____
    A. eliminate duplication of work
    B. overcome obstacles such as bad weather
    C. spot potential bottlenecks
    D. save on the cost of material

KEY (CORRECT ANSWERS)

1.	D	11.	C
2.	A	12.	B
3.	D	13.	B
4.	D	14.	C
5.	A	15.	D
6.	B	16.	D
7.	D	17.	A
8.	A	18.	A
9.	D	19.	A
10.	C	20.	C

21.	C
22.	D
23.	A
24.	C
25.	C

TEST 2

DIRECTIONS: Each question or incomplete statement is followed by several suggested answers or completions. Select the one that BEST answers the question or completes the statement. *PRINT THE LETTER OF THE CORRECT ANSWER IN THE SPACE AT THE RIGHT.*

1. Gantt refers to

   A. bar charts
   B. milestone charts
   C. PERT networks
   D. Management by Objectives

   1._____

2. PERT is an abbreviation for

   A. Progress Evaluation in Real Time
   B. Preliminary Evaluation of Running Time
   C. Program Evaluation Review Techniques
   D. Program Estimation and Repair Times

   2._____

3. In project management terms, slack is equivalent to

   A. tare   B. off time   C. delay   D. float

   3._____

4. The FIRST step in planning and programming a roadway pavement management system is to evaluate

   A. priorities for the work to be done
   B. the condition of your equipment
   C. the condition of the roads in the system
   D. the storage and maintenance facilities

   4._____

5. Managers accomplish their work in an ever changing environment by integrating three time-tested approaches. The one of the following that is NOT a time-tested approach is

   A. scientific adaptation
   B. scientific management
   C. behavior management
   D. management sciences

   5._____

6. The most effective managers manage for optimum results. This means that the manager is seeking to _____ a given situation.

   A. get the maximum results from
   B. get the most favorable results from
   C. get the most reasonable results from
   D. satisfy the conflicting interests in

   6._____

7. If a manager believes that an employee is irresponsible, the employee, in subtle response to the manager's assessment, will in fact prove to be irresponsible. This is an example of a(n)

   A. conditioned reflex
   B. self-fulfilling prophesy
   C. Freudian response
   D. automatic reaction

   7._____

8. Perhaps nothing distinguishes the younger generation from the older so much as the value placed on work. The older generation was generally raised to believe in the Protestant work ethic.
   This ethic holds primarily that

   8._____

A. people should try to get the highest salary possible
B. work should help people to advance
C. work should be well done if it is interesting
D. work is valuable in itself and the person who does it focuses on his work

9. The standard method currently in use in inspecting bituminous paving is to inspect each activity in detail as the paving work is being installed. In recent years some agencies use a different method of inspection known as a(n)

   A. as-built quality control method
   B. statistically controlled quality assurance method
   C. data based history of previous contracts of this type
   D. performance evaluation of the completed paving contract

9.____

10. Aggregates for use in bituminous pavements should be tested for grading,

    A. abrasion, soundness, and specific gravity
    B. type of rock, abrasion, and specific gravity
    C. abrasion, soundness, and deleterious material
    D. specific gravity, chemical composition of the aggregate, and deleterious material

10.____

11. Of the following, the one that is LEAST likely to be a test for asphalt is

    A. specific gravity   B. flashpoint
    C. viscosity   D. penetration

11.____

12. According to the AASHO, for bituminous pavements PSI is an abbreviation for _____ Index.

    A. Present Serviceability   B. Pavement Smoothness
    C. Pavement Serviceability   D. Present Smoothness

12.____

13. According to the AASHO, a bituminous pavement that is in extremely poor condition will have a PSI

    A. above 5.5   B. above 3.5
    C. below 3.5   D. below 1.5

13.____

14. The U.S. Federal Highway Administration defines asphalt maintenance as including work designed primarily for rejuvenation or protection of existing surfaces less than _____ inch minimum thickness.

    A. 1/4   B. 1/2   C. 3/4   D. 1

14.____

15. The maintenance phase of a highway management system includes the establishment of a program and schedule of work based largely on budget considerations, the actual operations of crack filling, patching, etc. and

    A. inspection of completed work
    B. planning of future operations
    C. upgrading existing pavements
    D. acquisition and processing of data

15.____

16. In a bituminous asphalt pavement, the progressive separation of aggregate particles in a pavement from the surface downward or from the edges inward is the definition of

    A. alligatoring
    B. raveling
    C. scaling
    D. disintegration

17. The bituminous pavement condition for the purpose of overlay design includes ride quality, structural capacity, skid resistance, and

    A. durability
    B. age of the pavement
    C. CBR value
    D. surface distress

18. An asphalt mix is being transferred from an asphalt truck to the hopper of the paving machine. Blue smoke rises from the material being emptied into the hopper of the paving machine.
    Your conclusion should be that

    A. this is normal and is to be expected
    B. the mix is overheated
    C. the mix is too cold
    D. the mix is being transferred too rapidly

19. Polished aggregate in an asphalt pavement are aggregate particles that have been rounded and polished smooth by traffic. This is a

    A. *good* condition as it allows a smooth ride
    B. *good* condition as it preserves tires
    C. *poor* condition as it promotes skidding
    D. *poor* condition as it tends to break the bond between the asphalt and the aggregate

20. A slippery asphalt surface requires a skid-resistant surfacing material. Of the following, the cover that would be most appropriate is a(n)

    A. asphalt tack coat
    B. fog seal
    C. layer of sand rolled into the asphalt surface
    D. asphalt emulsion slurry seal

21. The maximum size of aggregate in a hot mix asphalt concrete surfacing and bases allowed by the Federal Highway Administration Grading A is _____ inch(es).

    A. 3/4   B. 1   C. 1 1/4   D. 1 1/2

22. Wet sand weighs 132 pounds per cubic foot and contains 8% noisture. The dry weight of a cubic foot of sand is _____ pounds.

    A. 122.2   B. 122.0   C. 121.7   D. 121.4

23. A very light spray application of 551h emulsified asphalt diluted with water is used on existing pavement as a seal to riinimize raveling and to enrich the surface of a dried-out pavement is known as a(n)

    A. prime coat
    B. tack coat
    C. fog seal
    D. emulsion seal

24. 90 kilometers per hour is equivalent to _____ miles per hour. 24.____

　　A. 49　　　B. 54　　　C. 59　　　D. 64

25. In a table of pavement distress manifestations is a column broadly titled *Density of Pavement Distress*. 25.____
    This is equivalent to _____ of the defects.

　　A. average depth　　　　　B. average area
　　C. extent of occurrence　　D. seriousness

KEY (CORRECT ANSWERS)

1. A
2. A
3. D
4. C
5. A

6. B
7. B
8. D
9. B
10. C

11. A
12. A
13. D
14. C
15. D

16. B
17. D
18. B
19. C
20. D

21. D
22. A
23. C
24. B
25. C

EXAMINATION SECTION
TEST 1

DIRECTIONS: Each question or incomplete statement is followed by several suggested answers or completions. Select the one that BEST answers the question or completes the statement. *PRINT THE LETTER OF THE CORRECT ANSWER IN THE SPACE AT THE RIGHT.*

1. Reflective cracks in asphalt overlays

    A. are cracks in asphalt overlays that show the crack pattern of the pavement underneath
    B. are cracks that reflect caused by weakness in the base soil
    C. are the result of change in weights and frequency of truck travel in that they are greater than the loads the pavement was designed for
    D. reflect the type of cracks that normally could be expected for this type of pavement

   1.____

2. In a guide for the estimation of Pavement Condition Rating for asphalt concrete pavement on a highway is the following classification: *Pavement is in fairly good condition with frequent slight cracking or very slight channeling and a few areas with slight alligatoring. Rideability is fairly good with intermittent rough and uneven sections.*
   The maintenance recommendation for this class of pavement condition is

    A. no maintenance required
    B. normal maintenance only
    C. resurface in 3 to 5 years
    D. resurface within 3 years

   2.____

3. A major problem in bituminous asphalt plants is

    A. varying water content in the bituminous aggregate
    B. accuracy in the weighing equipment
    C. air pollution caused by plant exhausts
    D. producing a uniform mixture

   3.____

4. The primary difference between asphalt concrete and sheet asphalt is asphalt concrete

    A. uses a finer sand than sheet asphalt
    B. uses a lower viscosity asphalt than sheet asphalt
    C. generally has a thinner layer than sheet asphalt
    D. contains coarse aggregate whereas sheet asphalt does not have coarse aggregate

   4.____

5. It is common practice to apply a prime coat over untreated and some treated bases before asphalt concrete is placed. Of the following, the reasons for applying a prime coat are to

    A. bind loose particles of the base and minimize heat loss in the applied asphalt concrete
    B. act as a bond between base and pavement and prevent loss of asphalt in the asphalt concrete due to seepage
    C. deter rising moisture from penetrating the pavement and minimize heat loss in the applied asphalt concrete
    D. bind loose particles in the base and deter rising moisture from penetrating the asphalt pavement

   5.____

6. The asphalt content of open graded mixes is generally at

   A. the same level as dense graded asphalt
   B. a higher level than dense graded asphalt
   C. a lower level than dense graded asphalt
   D. at a higher or lower level than dense graded asphalt depending on the percent of fine aggregate in the open graded asphalt mix

7. Sheet asphalt was extensively used in the past with a thickness of _____ inch(es).

   A. 1/2　　　B. 3/4　　　C. 1　　　D. 1 1/2

8. The progressive separation of aggregate particles in a pavement from the surface downward or from the edges inward in an asphalt concrete pavement is known as

   A. raveling　　　　　　　　B. spalling
   C. scaling　　　　　　　　 D. reflective cracks

9. A profilometer used on an asphalt concrete road measures the _____ the road.

   A. grade of　　　　　　　　B. roughness of
   C. impact resistance of　　　D. channels in

10. Reinforcing steel is used in a footing. The minimum distance the bottom of the steel is above the subgrade should be _____ inch(es).

    A. 1　　　B. 2　　　C. 3　　　D. 4

11. Loose sand weighs 120 pounds per cubic foot and the specific gravity of sand is 2.65. The absolute volume of a cubic foot of loose sand is, in cubic feet, most nearly

    A. .73　　　B. .75　　　C. .77　　　D. .79

12. The maximum size of coarse aggregate in a concrete mix for a reinforced concrete structure is determined by the size of the concrete section and the

    A. type of cement used
    B. proportion of fine aggregate
    C. minimum distance between reinforcing bars
    D. yield point of the reinforcing steel

13. Cement (High Early Strength) is Type _____ cement.

    A. I　　　B. II　　　C. III　　　D. IV

14. Slunp in concrete is a measure of

    A. strength　　　　　B. porosity
    C. permeability　　　 D. workability

15. The cross section area of a #8 bar is _____ square inches.

    A. .60　　　B. .79　　　C. 1.00　　　D. 1.25

16. Construction joints for slabs in a building shall be made 16.____

   A. at the supports
   B. within 1/8 of the span of the slab from the supports
   C. from 1/8 to 3/8 of the span of the slab from the supports
   D. near the center of the span

17. Chutes for depositing concrete shall have a slope no greater than 17.____

   A. 1:1   B. 1:1½   C. 1:2   D. 1:2½

18. Air entrained cement is used in a concrete mix on highways primarily to 18.____

   A. make the concrete stronger after 28 days
   B. have a higher early strength
   C. make the surface more resistant to freezing and thawing
   D. make the surface less porous to better resist the impact of trucks

19. Beach sand is unsuitable as a fine aggregate in concrete because it has salt contamination and the sand particles are 19.____

   A. smooth   B. rough
   C. uniform in size D. too fine

20. The fineness modulus of sand for concrete is taken on the job to insure 20.____

   A. the quality of the sand
   B. that the gradation of the sand does not change
   C. that there is not an excess of fines in the sand
   D. that there is not an excess of oversized particles in the sand

21. The coarse and fine aggregate for concrete are usually tested 21.____

   A. at the quarry site
   B. at the job site
   C. by sampling a loaded truck
   D. in the design engineering office

22. The slump in concrete for highway mixtures range from _____ inches. 22.____

   A. 1 to 3   B. 2 to 5   C. 3 to 6   D. 4 to 7

23. A bag of cement weighs _____ pounds. 23.____

   A. 90   B. 94   C. 97   D. 100

24. The design strength of concrete is to be reached at the end of _____ days. 24.____

   A. 7   B. 14   C. 21   D. 28

25. Of the following, water-cement ratio may be defined as _____ of water per _____ of cement. 25.____

   A. gallons; bag   B. gallons; 100 pounds
   C. quarts; bag   D. quarts; 100 pounds

KEY (CORRECT ANSWERS)

1.	A	11.	A
2.	C	12.	C
3.	C	13.	C
4.	D	14.	D
5.	D	15.	B
6.	B	16.	D
7.	D	17.	C
8.	A	18.	C
9.	B	19.	C
10.	C	20.	B

21. A
22. A
23. B
24. D
25. A

TEST 2

DIRECTIONS: Each question or incomplete statement is followed by several suggested answers or completions. Select the one that BEST answers the question or completes the statement. *PRINT THE LETTER OF THE CORRECT ANSWER IN THE SPACE AT THE RIGHT.*

1. The maximum size of coarse aggregate in a concrete mix for a reinforced concrete structure is determined by the size of the section and the

   A. type of cement used
   B. proportion of fine aggregate
   C. minimum distance between reinforcing bars
   D. the yield point of the reinforcing steel

1.____

Questions 2-3.

DIRECTIONS: Questions 2 and 3 refer to concrete mix design.

2. The present and most popular method of rational mixture design is sponsored by ACI committee 211, 1994. In this method, the design using ordinary cement is based on

   A. slump and water-cement ratio
   B. aggregate size and water-cement ratio
   C. slump, aggregate size, and water-cement ratio
   D. slump and water content

2.____

3. In the method of mix design of ACI committee 211, 1994, water content is expressed in

   A. pounds of water per bag of cement
   B. pounds of water per cubic foot of concrete
   C. gallons of water per cubic yard of concrete
   D. pounds of water per cubic yard of concrete

3.____

4. The right to use or control the property of another for designated purposes is the definition of

   A. property acquisition   B. right-of-way
   C. an air right   D. an easement

4.____

5. A 24 inch circular drainage pipe is shown on a profile drawing of a highway as an ellipse with the major axis vertical. The reason for this is

   A. the horizontal and vertical scales of the profile drawing are different
   B. the pipe is not perpendicular to the center line of the roadway
   C. to emphasize the height of the pipe
   D. the slope of the pipe is taken into account

5.____

6. On a highway plan is a note for #4 wire game fence reading Lt Sta 2970 + 00 to 2979 + 85, Rt Sta 2970 + 00 to 2980 + 70. The total number of linear feet of new #4 wire game fence is, in feet, most nearly

   A. 1955   B. 2005   C. 2055   D. 2105

6.____

7. The superelevation of a curve is .075 feet. The superelevation, in inches, is most nearly   7._____
   A. 9   B. 5/8   C. 3/4   D. 7/8

8. On a plan for a highway is a note $\dfrac{\text{S.C.}}{\text{Sta 2968+56.50}}$ The S.C. is an abbreviation for   8._____
   A. slope at curve   B. spiral to circular curve
   C. superelevated curve   D. separation at center

9. Of the following methods of soil stabilization for the base of a highway pavement, the one that is most effective is   9._____
   A. a cement admixture
   B. a lime admixture
   C. an emulsified asphalt treated soil
   D. mechanical soil stabilization

10. An asphalt pavement mixture having a brownish dull appearance and lacking a shiny black luster   10._____
    A. is normal for an asphalt mixture
    B. contains too little aggregate
    C. is too cold
    D. contains too little asphalt

11. Steam rising from an asphalt mix when it is dumped into a hopper indicates   11._____
    A. there is excessive moisture in the aggregate
    B. the mix is overheated
    C. emulsification is taking place
    D. the mixture has not been adequately mixed

12. The disadvantage of excessive fine aggregate in an asphalt mix is   12._____
    A. it is difficult to get a uniform mix
    B. it will require an excessive amount of asphalt
    C. it is difficult to apply because of the grittiness of the mix
    D. the final surface will tend to be rough

13. On highways where heavy trucks are permitted, the percent of total traffic that are heavy trucks is, in percent, MOST NEARLY   13._____
    A. 4   B. 11   C. 18   D. 25

14. A single axle 80 kN load is equal to _____ pounds per axle.   14._____
    A. 12,000   B. 14,000   C. 16,000   D. 18,000

15. Normal traffic growth in the United States is _____ percent per year.   15._____
    A. 1-2   B. 3-5   C. 5-7   D. 7-9

16. EAL is an abbreviation for _____ axle load   16._____
    A. equal   B. equivalent
    C. effective   D. estimated

17. A roughometer is a single-wheeled trailer instrumented to measure the roughness of a pavement surface. The measure is in inches per 17._____

   A. foot B. yard C. hundred yards D. mile

18. The Atterberg Limit is a test on 18._____

   A. coarse aggregate B. asphalt
   C. soil D. Portland cement

19. Of the following, the one that is a high strength bolt is designated 19._____

   A. A7 B. A36 C. A180 D. A325

20. Construction contracts in a broad sense fall into two categories - fixed price and 20._____

   A. cost-plus B. fixed price plus overhead and profit
   C. negotiated price D. arbitrated price

21. A punch list on a construction job is usually made by the inspector 21._____

   A. weekly
   B. monthly
   C. continuously during the last half of the job
   D. near the end of the job

22. When an accident occurs on a construction job in which someone is injured, an accident report is usually made out by the 22._____

   A. insurance carrier B. contractor
   C. inspector D. inspector's superior

23. The inspector and the contractor share common goals. The one of the goals listed below that is NOT shared by the contractor and the inspector is 23._____

   A. get a good job done
   B. see that the contractor makes a reasonable profit
   C. get the job done as speedily as possible
   D. have the job done at as low a cost as possible

24. A crack relief layer is placed over an existing Portland cement concrete pavement followed by a well-graded intermediate course, then a dense graded surface course. The crack relief layer consists of an open graded 24._____

   A. mix of 100% crushed material with 25-35% interconnected voids
   B. crushed material heavily compacted with no binder
   C. hot mix made up of 80% crushed material with 20% shredded rubber
   D. dense crushed material with voids filled by asphalt

25. Most of the major work performed on the nation's bridges involves 25._____

   A. painting the bridges
   B. upgrading the bridges to carry heavier loads
   C. replacing the concrete decks
   D. replacing the suspenders on cable supported bridges

KEY (CORRECT ANSWERS)

1. C
2. C
3. D
4. D
5. A

6. C
7. D
8. B
9. A
10. D

11. A
12. B
13. B
14. D
15. B

16. B
17. D
18. C
19. D
20. A

21. D
22. B
23. B
24. A
25. C

EXAMINATION SECTION
TEST 1

DIRECTIONS: Each question or incomplete statement is followed by several suggested answers or completions. Select the one that BEST answers the question or completes the statement. *PRINT THE LETTER OF THE CORRECT ANSWER IN THE SPACE AT THE RIGHT.*

1. In pouring concrete for a large footing, the vibrator is used to move concrete into place. This is

    A. *good* practice as it moves the concrete quickly into place
    B. *good* practice as it eliminates air pockets
    C. *poor* practice as it promotes segregation
    D. *poor* practice as it increases pressure against the forms

    1.____

2. For successful winter work in placing ordinary concrete, adequate protection against the cold should be provided.
Special protection is NOT required when the temperature is over _____ and is required when the temperature is below _____.

    A. 50° F; 50° F
    B. 40° F; 40° F
    C. 30° F; 30° F
    D. 20° F; 20° F

    2.____

3. The MAIN reason for curing concrete is to

    A. prevent segregation of the concrete
    B. prevent the formation of air pockets in the concrete
    C. keep the concrete surface moist
    D. minimize bleeding in the poured concrete

    3.____

4. Of the following, the concrete mix that uses the greatest amount of cement per cubic yard of concrete is

    A. 1:2:4   B. 1:2:3 1/2   C. 1:2 1/2:5   D. 1:2 1/2:3 1/2

    4.____

5. The volume of concrete in a sidewalk 6 ft. x 30 ft. x 4 inches is, in cubic feet, MOST NEARLY

    A. 45   B. 50   C. 55   D. 60

    5.____

6. Of the following, the chemical compound that is added to a concrete mix to accelerate setting in cold weather is

    A. potassium chloride   B. calcium chloride
    C. sodium nitrate   D. calcium nitrate

    6.____

7. The compressive strength of concrete

    A. reaches a maximum after 28 days
    B. reaches a maximum after 90 days
    C. reaches a maximum after 180 days
    D. increases after 180 days

    7.____

8. The smallest size of coarse aggregate for concrete is, in inches, MOST NEARLY

   A. 1/4 B. 3/8 C. 1/2 D. 5/8

9. Of the following, the most practical way to determine that the water used in a concrete mix is satisfactory is

   A. send a sample to the laboratory
   B. taste the water
   C. the water is also used for drinking
   D. take a sample and let it stand for a while; and if no sediment at the bottom of the sample, it is satisfactory

10. Grout is

    A. cement, sand with water added so that it will flow readily
    B. cement with water added so that it is fluid
    C. cement and lime with water added so that it will flow readily
    D. gravel, sand, and lime with water added so that it will flow readily

11. Wire fabric has a designation 4 x 12 6/10. Of the following, the statement that is correct is the _____ center to enter and are _____.

    A. longitudinal wires are 12"; 10 gage
    B. longitudinal wires are 4"; 6 gage
    C. transverse wires are 4"; 6 gage
    D. transverse wires are 12; 6 gage

12. The volume of a bag of cement is _____ cubic foot(feet).

    A. 1 B. 1 1/2 C. 2 D. 2 1/2

13. The specifications state: *Forms for slabs shall be set with a camber of 1/4 inch for each 10 feet of span.* The purpose of this requirement is to

    A. compensate for deflection
    B. allow for small errors in setting the formwork
    C. allow for shrinkage of the concrete
    D. compensate for settlement of the supports for the formwork

14. When an inspector goes out to inspect the reinforcing steel before placing of the concrete, the most important drawings he should have with him are the _____ drawings.

    A. structural steel   B. reinforcing steel detail
    C. formwork   D. erection

15. A reinforcing bar has hooks at each end as shown at the right. The detail drawing of the bar will show dimension

    A. A
    B. B
    C. C
    D. D

16. Concrete sidewalks are usually finished with a

    A. screed B. steel float
    C. wood float D. darby

17. A new manhole consists of a concrete base made with ordinary cement and a brick superstructure. The minimum time that is usually required after the pouring of the concrete base to start the brickwork is _____ hours.

    A. 24 B. 48 C. 72 D. 96

18. In a new manhole, the slump in the concrete used in the base should be _____ inches.

    A. 2 to 3 B. 3 to 4 C. 4 to 5 D. 5 to 6

19. The dimensions of a cylinder used for testing the strength of concrete is _____ inch diameter and _____ inches high.

    A. 6; 9 B. 6; 12 C. 8; 9 D. 8; 12

20. The specification for the mixing time required for a concrete mix in a Ready-Mix truck is one minute for a one cubic yard batch and a quarter of a minute for every additional cubic yard. The minimum mixing time for a ten cubic yard batch is _____ minutes.

    A. 2 3/4 B. 3 C. 3 1/4 D. 3 1/2

21. The subgrade for a concrete footing is wetted down before concrete is poured into the footing.
    This is

    A. *poor* practice as the water-cement ratio of the concrete will be increased
    B. *poor* practice as it will leave a pocket on the underside of the footing
    C. *good* practice as the water-cement ratio of the concrete will be decreased
    D. *good* practice as the soil will not withdraw water from the concrete

22. Concrete should not be poured too rapidly into the formwork for thin walls primarily because

    A. segregation will result
    B. air pockets will form in the wall
    C. there will be excessive pressure on the formwork
    D. there will be seepage of water through the formwork.

23. The FIRST step in finishing the surface of a concrete pavement is

    A. darbying B. floating C. screeding D. tamping

24. The grade of a reinforcing steel is 40. The 40 represents the _____ of the steel.

    A. tensile strength B. ultimate strength
    C. yield point D. elastic limit

25. In reinforced concrete work, stirrups would MOST likely be found in

    A. beams B. columns C. walls D. footings

KEY (CORRECT ANSWERS)

1.	C	11.	B
2.	B	12.	A
3.	C	13.	A
4.	B	14.	B
5.	D	15.	D
6.	B	16.	C
7.	D	17.	A
8.	B	18.	A
9.	C	19.	B
10.	A	20.	C

21. D
22. C
23. C
24. C
25. A

TEST 2

DIRECTIONS: Each question or incomplete statement is followed by several suggested answers or completions. Select the one that BEST answers the question or completes the statement. *PRINT THE LETTER OF THE CORRECT ANSWER IN THE SPACE AT THE RIGHT.*

Questions 1-6.

DIRECTIONS: Questions 1 through 6, inclusive, refer to the following retaining wall.

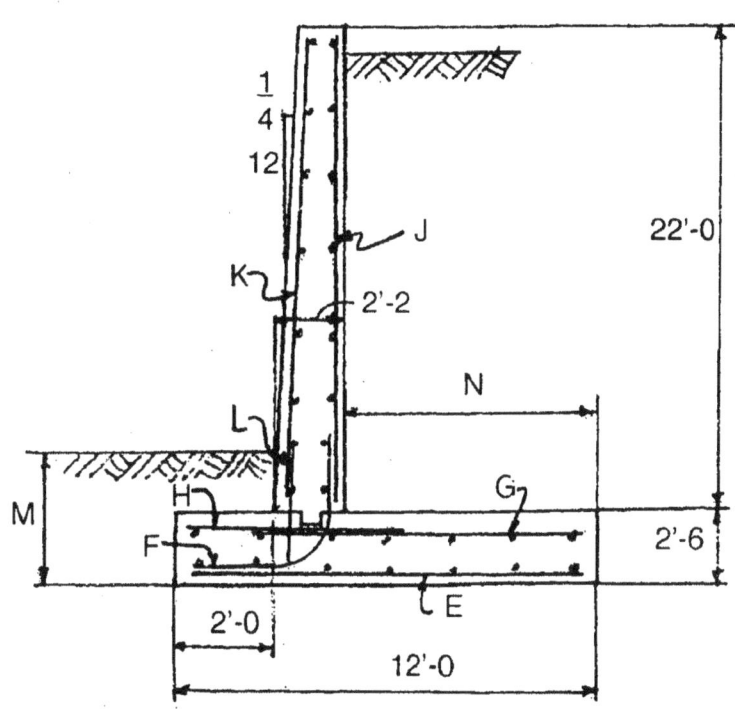

1. The largest size steel bars are most likely to be
   A. H, K, L B. E, F, J C. F, G, H D. F, G, J

2. Distance M is USUALLY at least
   A. 2'6" B. 3'0" C. 3'6" D. 4'0"

3. Dimension N is
   A. 7'6" B. 7'8" C. 7'10" D. 8'0"

4. The width of the wall at the top of the wall is
   A. 1'8" B. 1'8 1/2" C. 1'9" D. 1'9 1/2"

5. The volume of one foot of wall, in cubic feet, is most nearly (neglect the key at the bottom of the wall)
   A. 41.2 B. 41.7 C. 42.2 D. 42.6

23

6. The number of cubic yards of concrete in the footing fifty feet long is, in cubic yards, most nearly (neglect the key at the bottom of the wall)

    A. 54.6   B. 55.6   C. 56.6   D. 57.6

6.____

Questions 7-9.

DIRECTIONS: Questions 7 through 9, inclusive, refer to the markings on a reinforcing bar. The end of a reinforcing bar is marked H6N60.

7. The H in H6N60 indicates the

    A. method of treatment of the reinforcing bar
    B. hardness of the reinforcing steel bar
    C. initial of the steel mill
    D. type of steel in the reinforcing bar

7.____

8. The N in the reinforcing steel bar means

    A. new billet steel
    B. normalized reinforcing steel
    C. the area in which the steel has been produced (north east)
    D. the initial of the manufacturer

8.____

9. The 60 represents the

    A. ultimate strength of the steel
    B. diameter of the steel in millimeters
    C. allowable unit stress in the steel
    D. grade of the steel

9.____

10. The plywood industry produces a special product intended for concrete forming called

    A. structure ply   B. plyform
    C. formply   D. plycoat

10.____

11. Lumber that has been inspected and sorted will carry a grade stamp. The item LEAST likely to be found on the grade stamp is

    A. state of origin   B. grade
    C. species   D. condition of seasoning

11.____

12. In dimensioned lumber, wane indicates

    A. a lack of lumber
    B. narrow annular rings
    C. undersized width or length of lumber
    D. improper seasoning

12.____

13. A sidewalk slab is required to be 4" thick. Measuring down from a nail in the side form that represents the top of the slab, the distance is 4 1/2 inches. Of the following, the BEST action to take is

    A. have the contractor fill the subgrade with a half inch of sand
    B. have the contractor fill the subgrade with a half inch of grout

13.____

C. take no action as the contract requirement is met
D. point out the discrepancy to the contractor and ask him to take appropriate action

14. If high visibility is necessary on the job, a vest _____ colored should be worn.

    A. red   B. orange   C. yellow   D. green

15. Emulsified asphalt tack coats are preferred to using cut back asphalts PRIMARILY because

    A. cut-back asphalts present environmental problems
    B. cut-back asphalts are slower drying than emulsified asphalts
    C. cut-back asphalts are faster drying than emulsified asphalts
    D. emulsified asphalts are easier to place than cut-back asphalts

16. Spread footings are footings that

    A. cover a large area
    B. have an irregular shape
    C. are sometimes called strap footings
    D. transmit their loads through a combination of piles and soil

17. An excavation for a footing is over-excavated and the subgrade is well below the design elevation. Of the following, the BEST action for the contractor to take is

    A. fill the excavation with well compacted soil until it reaches the design elevation of the bottom of the footing
    B. fill the subgrade with gravel to reach the bottom elevation of the footing
    C. lower the elevation of the footing but retain its thickness
    D. change the footing to a pile supported footing

18. The inspector should be aware of the items in the contract that are unit price so that he can

    A. make the proper inspection of these items
    B. keep a record of when they are delivered to the job site
    C. make measurements and compute quantities that may be necessary
    D. record the dates of installation of these items

19. The attitudes that an inspector should adopt in dealing with the contractor are to be

    A. understanding and flexible
    B. helpful and cautious
    C. cautious and skeptical
    D. firm and fair

20. Among the provisions for the safety of workers on the job, the most basic and general one is

    A. workmen should work slowly
    B. keep alcohol off the job
    C. good housekeeping
    D. wear suitable clothing for extreme weather conditions

21. Ladders should extend a minimum of _____ above the level to which they lead. 21._____
    A. six feet
    B. knee-high
    C. waist-high
    D. five feet

22. An inspector notices a worker working in an unsafe manner. Of the following, the BEST action the inspector can take is to 22._____
    A. tell the worker the correct way to work
    B. tell the worker's supervisor of the unsafe behavior of the worker
    C. record the incident in your log book
    D. notify the contractor so that the unsafe practice will cease

23. In making the daily report, personal remarks by the inspector should not be included. Of the following, the best reason for this exclusion is 23._____
    A. it may raise questions as to the accuracy of the report
    B. the wrong people may read the daily report
    C. the inspector should have no opinions
    D. it may indicate bias on the part of the inspector

24. The major difference between a softwood and a hardwood in forestry terms is 24._____
    A. the softwoods are from the south and the hardwoods are from the north
    B. the softwoods are evergreens and the hardwoods are deciduous
    C. the softwoods are soft and the hardwoods are hard
    D. there is one grading method for softwoods and another grading method for hardwoods

25. Lumber is considered unseasoned if it has a moisture content of not less than _____ percent in weight of water. 25._____
    A. 17
    B. 20
    C. 23
    D. 26

KEY (CORRECT ANSWERS)

1. D
2. D
3. C
4. B
5. D

6. B
7. C
8. A
9. D
10. B

11. A
12. A
13. C
14. B
15. A

16. A
17. A
18. C
19. D
20. C

21. C
22. B
23. D
24. B
25. B

EXAMINATION SECTION
TEST 1

DIRECTIONS: Each question or incomplete statement is followed by several suggested answers or completions. Select the one that BEST answers the question or completes the statement. *PRINT THE LETTER OF THE CORRECT ANSWER IN THE SPACE AT THE RIGHT.*

1. Asphalt is derived mainly

    A. as a byproduct from the production of coke
    B. from asphalt deposits seeping to the surface of the earth
    C. from the refining of crude oil
    D. from bituminous coal

    1.____

2. Cutback liquid asphalts are prepared by blending asphalt with a volatile solvent. The one of the following that is NOT used as an asphalt solvent is

    A. naphtha   B. gasoline   C. kerosene   D. toluene

    2.____

3. The primary purpose of the solvent in cutback asphalt is to allow the

    A. use of a larger size aggregate in the mix
    B. application of the asphalt at a relatively low temperature
    C. application of asphalt in wet weather
    D. application of asphalt in hot weather

    3.____

4. The thickness of the sheet asphalt on a sheet asphalt pavement is usually _____ inch(es).

    A. 1/2 inch to 3/4   B. 1 inch to 1 1/2
    C. 1 5/8 inches to 2   D. 2 1/4 inches to 3

    4.____

5. The grade of an asphalt cement is designated as AR4000.
   The AR is an abbreviation for

    A. asphalt rating   B. acid resistance
    C. aged residue   D. aging resistance

    5.____

6. An asphaltic emulsion is a suspension of asphalt in

    A. kerosene   B. gasoline   C. toluene   D. water

    6.____

7. A very light application of asphalt on an existing paved surface will promote bond between this surface and the subsequent course is known as a(n) _____ coat.

    A. prime   B. adhesion
    C. tack   D. penetrating

    7.____

8. Of the following, payment is usually made for asphalt pavements at the contract price per

    A. square inch   B. square foot
    C. square yard   D. 100 square feet

    8.____

29

9. The grade of an asphalt cement is designated AR4000. The 4000 is a measure of

   A. strength B. viscosity C. ductility D. density

10. Of the following, the geometric shape of a horizontal curve on a highway is

    A. parabolic
    B. hyperbolic
    C. circular
    D. elliptical

11. A borrow pit in highway construction is used

    A. for storing stormwater in a heavy rain
    B. for coarse aggregate in Portland cement concrete
    C. for coarse aggregate in asphalt concrete
    D. to obtain fill for embankments

12. Overhaul in highway construction is usually measured and paid for by the

    A. yard - cubic foot
    B. yard - cubic yard
    C. station - cubic foot
    D. station - cubic yard

13. A Benkelman beam is used in highway work

    A. as an indicator of the ability of a pavement to withstand loading
    B. to measure the roughness of an asphalt concrete pavement
    C. to measure the uniformity of an asphalt concrete pavement
    D. to measure the ability of an asphalt concrete pavement to remain serviceable if the subgrade is undermined

14. When surfacing over an existing pavement, of the following, the MOST practical way to insure that the required thickness of new pavement is met is

    A. expansion of clay when exposed to water
    B. expansion of soil when excavated
    C. waviness in a soil embankment when being compacted with a roller
    D. expansion of loamy soil when exposed to water

15. When surfacing over an existing pavement, of the following, the MOST practical way to insure that the required thickness of new pavement is met is

    A. have wood blocks of the thickness of the new pavement temporarily placed on the existing pavement to insure that the thickness requirements will be met at the time of paving
    B. make a survey of the existing pavement elevations and a survey of the final pavement elevations and check that the thickness requirements are met
    C. check that the amount of asphalt delivered is adequate to meet the depth requirements of the area to be paved
    D. take core borings to determine if the thickness meets specifications

16. The maximum roller speed for steel tired rollers paving asphalt concrete is a maximum of _____ mile(s) per hour.

    A. 7 B. 5 C. 3 D. 1

17. The weathered or dry surface appearing on a relatively new pavement can generally be attributed to   17.____

    A. inadequate rolling
    B. oversized coarse aggregate in the mix
    C. excessive amount of fine aggregate
    D. insufficient asphalt in the mix

18. Construction contracts for highways have items paid either by unit price or lump sum. The one of the following that is usually a lump sum item on a highway contract is   18.____

    A. excavation   B. paving
    C. fencing   D. demolition

19. Highway roadway subgrades are usually required to have a relative density of _____ percent.   19.____

    A. 80 to 84   B. 85 to 89   C. 90 to 95   D. 100

20. A *profile* of a highway is   20.____

    A. the section taken along the centerline of the highway
    B. an aesthetic landscape sketch of the highway
    C. used to determine the line of the highway
    D. used to locate overpasses

21. A culvert as used under a highway is usually installed   21.____

    A. as a relief sewer
    B. as a bypass for a stream
    C. in a stream bed
    D. to carry sanitary and storm flow

22. A mass diagram as related to highway construction work is used to   22.____

    A. minimize traffic congestion
    B. compute payment for hauling excavation and fill
    C. find the largest feasible radius of curvature for a horizontal curve
    D. help determine the depth of an asphalt concrete pavement

23. The geometric shape of a vertical curve on a highway is a(n)   23.____

    A. parabola   B. hyperbola   C. circle   D. ellipse

24. When cast iron bell and spigot pipe is used in sewer construction, the joint is usually sealed with   24.____

    A. lead   B. tin
    C. cement mortar   D. oakum

25. A planimeter is used to measure   25.____

    A. location   B. area   C. elevation   D. angles

KEY (CORRECT ANSWERS)

1. C
2. D
3. B
4. B
5. C

6. D
7. C
8. B
9. B
10. C

11. D
12. D
13. A
14. B
15. A

16. C
17. D
18. D
19. C
20. A

21. C
22. B
23. A
24. A
25. B

TEST 2

DIRECTIONS: Each question or incomplete statement is followed by several suggested answers or completions. Select the one that BEST answers the question or completes the statement. *PRINT THE LETTER OF THE CORRECT ANSWER IN THE SPACE AT THE RIGHT.*

1. A witness stake is usually used in surveying primarily as

   A. proof that a given location has been surveyed
   B. an aid in locating a surveying stake
   C. a marker to prevent a stake being disturbed
   D. an offset stake

2. Before the contractor begins work on a sewer or highway project, a detailed survey is made of all existing structures that may be affected by the construction in order to

   A. protect against false claims for damage
   B. insure that the contractor causes no damage to property
   C. insure that existing elevations conform to elevations on the contract drawings
   D. uncover potential weaknesses in structures

3. The optimum moisture content of a given soil will result in the

   A. plastic limit of the soil is reached
   B. liquid limit of the soil is reached
   C. porosity of the soil is at its maximum
   D. soil is compacted to its maximum dry density

4. The letters SC for soil means

   A. silty clay
   B. clayey sand
   C. sandy clay
   D. clayey silt

5. A cradle is used under a large precast circular concrete pipe sewer. The purpose of the cradle is mainly to

   A. minimize the settlement of the earth on the sides of the sewer
   B. minimize the settlement under the pipe
   C. strengthen the pipe against collapse
   D. resist side pressure against the pipe

6. The joints on laid precast concrete pipe were poorly made.
   The consequence of this poor workmanship is most likely

   A. the pipe will settle
   B. the pipe may collapse
   C. the water table may be adversely affected
   D. there will be excessive infiltration

7. An existing sewer is to connect into a new deep manhole for a new sewer. According to old plans for the existing sewer, the elevation of the existing sewer is 1/2 inch lower than shown on the plan.
   Of the following, the BEST action that the inspector can take is

A. call his superior for instructions
B. do nothing
C. have the contractor relay the existing pipe to the theoretical elevation shown on the old plan
D. have an adjustable connection placed between the old pipe and the new manhole

8. The contractor proposes using a cement-lime mix for cement mortar to be used in building a manhole.
   This is

   A. *good* practice as this is a more workable mortar
   B. *good* practice as the mortar is slow setting
   C. *poor* practice because the mortar weakens in a wet environment
   D. *poor* practice as a cement-lime mortar is more porous than a cement mortar

9. Most serious claims for extra payment on large sewer contracts result from

   A. soil conditions that are markedly different from those that were presented by the owner
   B. the inspectors being unreasonable in their demands
   C. delay in making the areas available for work
   D. the fact that the method of construction required by the owner proved to be unworkable

10. Unconsolidated fill is at pipe laying depth. Of the following, the BEST action that an inspector can take is to

    A. have the unconsolidated fill removed and replaced with concrete
    B. have the unconsolidated fill removed and replaced with sound fill
    C. report this matter to your supervisor for his consideration
    D. ask the contractor to consolidate the fill

11. Buried debris not shown on the borings is uncovered near the surface of an excavation for a deep sewer. Of the following, the BEST action for an inspector to take is to

    A. record the depth and extent of the debris in the event of a claim
    B. do nothing as this has no effect on the final product
    C. notify the contractor that there is no valid claim for the extra work required
    D. be certain that the debris is not used in the backfill

12. A come-along or deadman is sometimes used in the laying of large precast concrete pipe to insure

    A. the pipe is at proper grade
    B. the pipe is on proper line
    C. that the pipe will not subsequently settle
    D. that the pipe is properly seated

13. In laying sewers,

    A. accuracy in the line of the sewer is more important than accuracy in the grade of the sewer
    B. accuracy in the grade of the sewer is more important than accuracy in the line of the sewer

C. accuracy in the line and grade of the sewer are equally important
D. since the sewer is underground, accuracy is not required either for line or grade

14. A sewer contract is given out with a price per foot of sewer for different diameter sewers. After the contract is let, the low bidder is required to give a breakdown of his price per foot of sewer to include excavation, sewer in place, backfill, and restoration. The purpose of this breakdown is to 14.____

    A. facilitate partial payments
    B. insure the bid is not unbalanced
    C. enable the agency to gather up-to-date cost data for future projects
    D. make it easier to price extra work

15. The house sewer runs from the house to the main line sewer. The size of this sewer is most frequently _____ inches. 15.____

    A. 4   B. 5   C. 6   D. 8

16. A line on centerline at the inside bottom of a pipe or conduit is known as the 16.____

    A. convert   B. invert   C. subvert   D. exvert

17. One of the most important elements of excavating for sewer construction is to maintain the specified width of the trench at the top of the pipe. If the width at the top of the pipe is too great, 17.____

    A. this may cause excessive settlement of the pipe
    B. this may cause excessive settlement of the backfill damaging the final pavement
    C. this may place excessive load on the pipe
    D. it may undermine utilities adjacent to the pipe

18. Wellpoints are used in sewer construction mainly to 18.____

    A. keep water out of the trench due to a heavy rainstorm
    B. keep water out of the excavation and subsoil to avoid excessive pressure on the sheeting
    C. prevent a boil from forming in the trench
    D. lower the water table to facilitate construction of the sewer

19. When a trench excavation uses soldier beams and horizontal sheeting for support, the minimum number of braces for each soldier beam is 19.____

    A. 1   B. 2   C. 3   D. 4

20. Bell and spigot pipe should be laid _____ with the bell end pointed _____. 20.____

    A. downstream; upstream   B. downstream; downstream
    C. upstream; upstream   D. upstream; downstream

21. The specifications state that house sewers should be laid at a grade of not less than 2%. In 40 feet of house sewer, the change in grade for 40 feet should be most nearly _____ inches. 21.____

    A. 8   B. 8 1/2   C. 9   D. 9 1/2

22. Two percent grade on a house sewer is equal to most nearly _____ inch per foot. 22._____

    A. 1/8   B. 3/16   C. 1/4   D. 5/16

23. When working underground in spaces that are closed and confined, such as manholes, the gas that is dangerous and most likely of the following to be present is 23._____

    A. carbon monoxide   B. carbon dioxide
    C. ammonia   D. methane

24. Of the following, air entrained cement would most likely be used in 24._____

    A. concrete roadways
    B. precast concrete pipe
    C. precast concrete manholes
    D. the cradle for precast concrete pipe

25. A slump cone is filled to overflowing in _____ layer(s). 25._____

    A. one   B. two separate
    C. three separate   D. four separate

KEY (CORRECT ANSWERS)

1.	B		11.	A
2.	A		12.	D
3.	D		13.	B
4.	B		14.	A
5.	B		15.	C
6.	D		16.	B
7.	B		17.	C
8.	C		18.	D
9.	A		19.	B
10.	C		20.	C

21. D
22. C
23. D
24. A
25. C

EXAMINATION SECTION
TEST 1

DIRECTIONS: Each question or incomplete statement is followed by several suggested answers or completions. Select the one that BEST answers the question or completes the statement. *PRINT THE LETTER OF THE CORRECT ANSWER IN THE SPACE AT THE RIGHT.*

1. On the monthly report of the amount of work completed, the units used to measure the amount of work completed on guardrails and beam barriers installed on arterial highways is

    A. square feet
    B. square yards
    C. linear feet
    D. linear yards

2. On the daily work report for the sidewalk concrete gang is a formula, $M = [G - (D + U)]$, where G = total man-hours worked, D = total man-hours delays, U = total man-hours unmeasured work, and M = total man-hours measured work.
If G = 98, D = 42, U = 21, then M is equal to

    A. 35   B. 56   C. 77   D. 119

3. When a plumber *opens a street*, he is responsible for restoring the pavement. After completion of the permanent restoration, the plumber is responsible for maintaining the restored area for a total period of

    A. six months
    B. one year
    C. one year and 6 months
    D. two years

4. A permit for a street opening may be issued for a single permit activity for one block length up to a MAXIMUM length of _____ feet.

    A. 50   B. 100   C. 200   D. 300

5. A street obstruction bond taken out by a contractor working in the street is to insure the city if

    A. a pedestrian is injured by material stored on the sidewalk
    B. an automobile is damaged by material stored in the street
    C. curbs, sidewalks, and pavements are damaged
    D. obstructions, illegally placed in the street, must be removed

6. On the daily work report for the sidewalk concrete gang is an item *curb*.
The different types of curb listed on the report are: bluestone or granite, concrete-steel face, concrete-regular face, and

    A. drop
    B. paving block
    C. concrete block
    D. prefabricated

7. On the monthly report of work output under time (manhours) is a column headed MSO, which refers to manhours

    A. of mechanical services operator other than MVO
    B. of operation time lost while waiting
    C. of operation time lost due to the weather
    D. spent operating mechanical equipment by the MVO

8. In the city, concrete sidewalks are required to have a minimum thickness of concrete of _____ inches.

   A. 3   B. 4   C. 5   D. 6

9. Asphalt was laid for a length of 210 feet on the entire width of a street whose curb-to-curb distance is 30 feet. The number of square yards covered with asphalt is MOST NEARLY

   A. 210   B. 700   C. 2100   D. 6300

10. A layer of cinders is used as a base for a concrete sidewalk.
    The MAIN purpose of the cinders is to

    A. act as an air entraining agent for the concrete in the sidewalk
    B. replace poor soil under the sidewalk
    C. provide drainage under the sidewalk
    D. cushion the sidewalk when heavy loads are placed on the sidewalk

11. The unit used on the daily gang report to report the amount of measurement of debris removed is

    A. square foot   B. square yard
    C. cubic foot   D. cubic yard

12. 627 cubic feet contains MOST NEARLY _____ cubic yards.

    A. 21   B. 22   C. 23   D. 24

13. Of the following, the one that is INCORRECT curb construction is a curb made

    A. with a height of 5 inches
    B. with a steel angle for the face
    C. without a steel face
    D. monolithically with the sidewalk

14. Where feasible, concrete sidewalk panels should be made in squares of _____ feet by _____ feet.

    A. 3; 3   B. 5; 5   C. 6; 6   D. 7; 7

15. The steel facing for concrete curbs are splayed

    A. at an expansion joint
    B. where it butts against an adjacent steel plate
    C. at a drop curb
    D. at a radius bend

16. Expansion joints in steel curb facing shall be 1/4 inch wide and shall be filled with

    A. sand   B. premolded filler
    C. poured asphalt   D. dry pack

17. One inch is MOST NEARLY equal to _____ feet.

    A. 0.8   B. 0.08   C. 0.008   D. 0.0008

18. Of the following, the *final* finish on a sidewalk is MOST frequently made with a

    A. wood float
    B. screed
    C. steel trowel
    D. darby

19. An air entraining compound would be added to concrete MAINLY to

    A. make the concrete lighter
    B. make the concrete cure faster
    C. improve the resistance of the concrete to frost action
    D. increase the tensile strength of the concrete

20. *ASTM,* as used in specifications for concrete, is an abbreviation for the

    A. American Society for Testing Materials
    B. American Standard Training Manual
    C. American Standard Testing Materials
    D. Association of Scientists for Testing Materials

21. A 15-foot-wide sidewalk has a pitch of 1/4 inch per foot. The difference in elevation from the curb to 15 feet from the curb in the direction of the pitch is _____ inches.

    A. 3   B. 3 3/4   C. 4   D. 4 1/2

22. A liquid asphalt is designated *RC70.*
    The letters RC stand for

    A. Rough Course
    B. Rubber Cement
    C. Rapid Curing
    D. Reinforced Concrete

23. Unless otherwise specified, steel faced concrete curb shall consist of the steel curb facing in _____-foot lengths.

    A. 5   B. 10   C. 15   D. 20

24. The difference between sheet asphalt and asphaltic concrete is that sheet asphalt

    A. contains no sand while asphaltic concrete contains sand
    B. contains no coarse aggregate while asphaltic concrete contains coarse aggregate
    C. contains no mineral filler while asphaltic concrete contains mineral filler
    D. has no flux while asphaltic concrete has flux

25. An approved roller shall weigh not less than 225 pounds per inch width of main roll. If the main roll width is 60 inches, the MINIMUM roller weight shall be equal to or greater than _____ lbs.

    A. 12,000   B. 12,500   C. 13,000   D. 13,500

KEY (CORRECT ANSWERS)

1.	C	11.	D
2.	A	12.	C
3.	D	13.	D
4.	D	14.	B
5.	C	15.	C
6.	A	16.	B
7.	A	17.	B
8.	B	18.	A
9.	B	19.	C
10.	C	20.	A

21. B
22. C
23. D
24. B
25. D

TEST 2

DIRECTIONS: Each question or incomplete statement is followed by several suggested answers or completions. Select the one that BEST answers the question or completes the statement. *PRINT THE LETTER OF THE CORRECT ANSWER IN THE SPACE AT THE RIGHT.*

1. A specification states that the rate of application of asphalt cement shall be 1 1/2 gallons per square yard with a tolerance of 1/10 of a gallon.
   Of the following, the rate of application that would be acceptable is _____ gallons per square yard.

   A. 1.2   B. 1.3   C. 1.6   D. 1.7

2. Of the following, the BEST reason for compacting backfill is to

   A. prevent settlement   B. crush oversized rocks
   C. facilitate drainage   D. make the soil uniform

3. Asphalt block is hexagonal tile block.
   The number of vertical sides of each block in place is

   A. 4   B. 6   C. 8   D. 10

4. Concrete driveways shall have a MINIMUM thickness of concrete of _____ inches.

   A. 5   B. 6   C. 7   D. 8

5. When the tops of manholes must be raised because of repaving, the MOST practical of the following methods to use is to

   A. break out the manhole frame and replace it with a deeper frame
   B. remove the manhole frame, build up the top of the manhole with bricks, and reset the frame
   C. use a thicker manhole cover
   D. place a metal collar on top of the existing frame

6. In a 1:2:4 concrete mix, the 2 indicates the quantity of

   A. water   B. sand   C. cement   D. aggregate

7. A tree pit shall be located in the area immediately in back of the curb.
   The MAXIMUM size of the tree pit shall be

   A. 3' x 3'   B. 4' x 4'   C. 5' x 5'   D. 6' x 6'

8. A temporary asphaltic pavement is placed over an excavation in the street by a private contractor.
   The MINIMUM required thickness of the finish course of the temporary asphaltic pavement is _____ inch(es).

   A. 1   B. 2   C. 3   D. 4

9. When a vault is abandoned, it must be filled in with clean incombustible materials, well-tamped.
   Where such structures adjoin the curb of a street, the roof must be removed and the enclosing walls cut down below the curb to a depth of _____ feet.

   A. 2   B. 4   C. 6   D. 8

10. Granite curbs are required to be set on a cradle. The MAIN purpose of the cradle is to

    A. prevent cracking of the curb
    B. prevent settling of the curb
    C. help keep the curb in line while it is being set
    D. separate the curb from the adjacent sidewalk

11. Paving was installed on a street from Station 3+15 to Station 4+90.
    The length of street that was paved is _____ feet.

    A. 75   B. 115   C. 175   D. 215

12. A district foreman uses an engineer's tape and measures a distance of 26.50 feet.
    This distance is equal to _____ feet _____ inch(es).

    A. 26; 5   B. 26; 6   C. 26; 1/2   D. 26; 0.6

13. Written on a can containing material delivered from a manufacturer is the notation *Approved by the B.S. & A.*
    The B.S. & A. is an abbreviation for the

    A. Bureau of Shipping and Allocation
    B. Board of Standards and Appeals
    C. Board of Supervision and Approval
    D. Bureau of Supervision and Assistance

14. An asphalt macadam pavement consists of a base course and a wearing course. The purpose of the base course is to

    A. provide drainage
    B. provide a level surface for the wearing course
    C. spread the load from the surface when it reaches the soil
    D. replace defective soil

15. Of the following, the MOST important recent advancement in power-driven equipment and tools is

    A. reduction in weight of the equipment
    B. improved surface finish
    C. higher operating speed
    D. lower noise levels

16. A wooden horse, used to warn traffic away, should be placed in front of which of the following defects in the street?
    A

    A. broken curb
    B. piece of roadway pavement that is very thin and the pavement whose base is starting to show through
    C. very badly broken manhole cover in the center of the street
    D. catch basin filled to the surface with debris

17. When a street is to be paved, the roller should 17.____

    A. start at the curb, go the length of the street and then move toward the center
    B. move from curb to curb transversely across the street
    C. start at the center, go the length of the street, and then move toward the curb
    D. roll at all the manhole covers first and then start rolling the length of the street

18. The use of long chutes to place concrete for a road base is usually prohibited. 18.____
    The BEST of the following reasons for prohibiting long chutes in this case is that

    A. the concrete will set by the time it is in place
    B. the water will evaporate from the mix
    C. segregation of the aggregate will occur
    D. the stone will be broken down into smaller particles

19. When sheet asphalt is spread by hand, the speed of the rolling should NOT exceed 19.____
    _____ square yards per hour.

    A. 100   B. 300   C. 500   D. 700

20. Of the following, the BEST way to insure long trouble-free operation of mechanical equipment is by periodic inspection and 20.____

    A. use   B. servicing
    C. painting   D. rotation of operators

21. Of the following maintenance work, the one type that is LEAST likely to be done by your agency on mechanical equipment is 21.____

    A. tune-up   B. repairing
    C. overhauling   D. rebuilding

22. Of the following, the MOST important equipment needed to lay sheet asphalt pavement is truck, roller, fire wagon, and 22.____

    A. grader   B. distributor
    C. planer   D. spreader

23. Of the following, the BEST reason why deep potholes should be repaired *immediately* is that 23.____

    A. they look bad
    B. they are a safety hazard
    C. they present a drainage problem
    D. people complaining about unfilled potholes cause unfavorable publicity

24. Of the following, the MOST serious safety hazard on highway and street maintenance work is 24.____

    A. injury from flying debris during pavement breaking
    B. motor traffic
    C. working close to trucks, bulldozers, and rollers
    D. cave-ins

25. Of the following, the BEST way a laborer can avoid accidents is to

    A. work slowly
    B. be alert
    C. wear safety shoes
    D. wear glasses

26. Of the following, the BEST first aid treatment for a second degree burn is to cover the burn with a _____ sterile dressing.

    A. thin, wet
    B. thin, dry
    C. thick, wet
    D. thick, dry

27. One of the laborers on the job feels unusually tired, has a headache and nausea, is perspiring heavily, and the skin is pale and clammy.
    He is probably suffering from

    A. epilepsy
    B. food poisoning
    C. heat exhaustion
    D. sunstroke

28. If a laborer feels faint, the BEST advice to give him is to advise him to

    A. lie flat with his head low
    B. walk around till he revives
    C. run around till he revives
    D. drink a glass of cold water

29. Of the following types of fire extinguisher, the one to use on an electrical fire is

    A. soda acid
    B. carbon dioxide
    C. water pump tank
    D. pyrene

30. The GREATEST number of injuries from equipment used in construction work result from

    A. carelessness of the operator
    B. poor maintenance of the equipment
    C. overloading of the equipment
    D. poor inspection of the equipment

KEY (CORRECT ANSWERS)

1. C
2. A
3. B
4. C
5. D

6. B
7. C
8. C
9. A
10. B

11. C
12. B
13. B
14. C
15. D

16. C
17. A
18. C
19. B
20. B

21. D
22. D
23. B
24. B
25. B

26. D
27. C
28. A
29. B
30. A

EXAMINATION SECTION
TEST 1

DIRECTIONS: Each question or incomplete statement is followed by several suggested answers or completions. Select the one that BEST answers the question or completes the statement. *PRINT THE LETTER OF THE CORRECT ANSWER IN THE SPACE AT THE RIGHT.*

1. 0.8021 feet is, in inches, MOST NEARLY

    A. 9 1/4   B. 9 3/8   C. 9 1/2   D. 9 5/8

2. The structural steel shape MOST often used as a stair stringer is a

    A. channel   B. angle   C. tee   D. zee

3. The abbreviation M.S.L. appearing on a topographic map means

    A. measure straight lengths
    B. make side longer
    C. mean sea level
    D. most safe lintel

4. A specification for sand to be used in concrete requires that sand be well graded. *Well graded* means that the particles be

    A. minute   B. coarse
    C. of variable sizes   D. of one size

5. A vertical transverse profile in a street showing the underground utilities is called a(n) _____-section.

    A. cross   B. contour   C. invert   D. front

6. The seepage of ground water into a sewer line is known as

    A. ingestion   B. infiltration
    C. attrition   D. dilution

7. The number of board feet in 15 pieces of 2' x 6" x 12' feet of lumber is

    A. 180   B. 360   C. 1080   D. 2160

8. The diameter of pipe, in inches, required to carry a flow of 1200 G.P.M. at a velocity of 4.91 f.p.s. is MOST NEARLY (7.48 gal. =1 cu.ft.)

    A. 8   B. 10   C. 12   D. 14

9. If the thickness of the steel wall of a 24 inch diameter water main is 1/2 inch and the water pressure in the water main is 125 p.s.i., then the unit stress in the steel, in p.s.i., is MOST NEARLY

    A. 1500   B. 2000   C. 2500   D. 3000

10. An interior angle of a five-sided traverse is measured six times and recorded as 250°55'30".
    The angle is MOST NEARLY

    A. 40°12'30"   B. 40°18'5"   C. 41°19'15"   D. 41°49'15"

11. The total number of square feet of floor area in three rooms whose measurements are 12'8" x 10'0", 10'2" x 11'8", and 12'5" x 13'8", respectively, is MOST NEARLY

    A. 410   B. 415   C. 420   D. 425

Questions 12-13.

DIRECTIONS: Questions 12 and 13 refer to the following surveying leveling notes.

STA	BS	HI	FS	ELEV
BM_1	6.23'			84.47'
TP_1	5.67'		8.29'	
TP_2	7.48'		3.41'	
BM_2			4.53'	

12. The HI of BM_1 is, in feet,

    A. 77.24   B. 79.36   C. 87.58   D. 89.70

13. The ELEV TP_2 is, in feet,

    A. 82.59   B. 83.67   C. 85.70   D. 87.18

14. A #6 bar has an area equivalent to a circle whose diameter is

    A. 1/4"   B. 1/2"   C. 3/4"   D. 1"

15.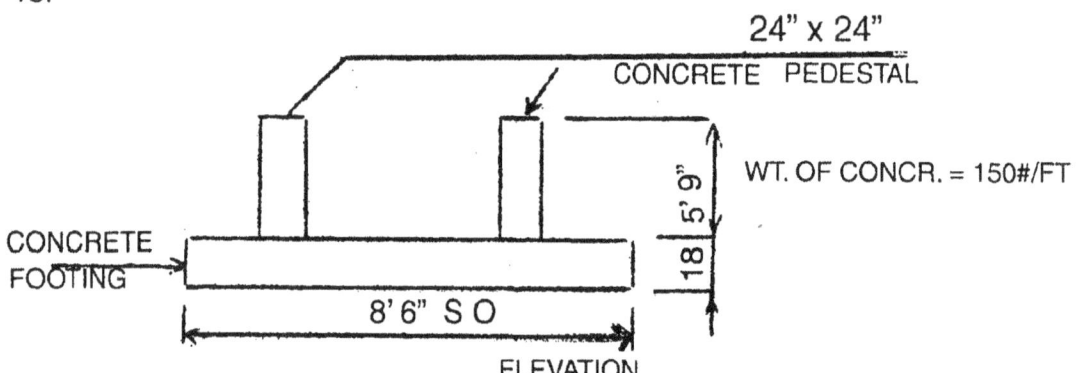

    The total weight, in pounds, of the above concrete footing and pedestal is MOST NEARLY

    A. 20,200   B. 23,100   C. 32,600   D. 41,500

16. The capacity, in gallons, of a flat head steel tank 38 inches in diameter by five feet long is MOST NEARLY (7.5 gal. = 1 cu.ft.)

    A. 250   B. 275   C. 295   D. 315

17. The drafting symbol ——⊳⊲—— on a piping drawing indicates a _____ valve.

    A. globe   B. butterfly
    C. check   D. pressure relief

18. If the floor to floor height in a building is 9'6" and there are 15 equal risers, then the height of each riser is, in inches, MOST NEARLY

    A. 7.3   B. 7.4   C. 7.5   D. 7.6

19. A 2,200 feet long pipeline, 18 I.D., carries water at 5.06 feet per second. If the f is 0.02, then the total loss in head due to friction in the pipeline, in feet of water, is MOST NEARLY ($hf = flv^2/d2g$)

    A. 9.4   B. 10.5   C. 11.6   D. 12.3

20.

    The cross bracing labeled X on the ELEVATION shown above is called

    A. bridging   B. studding   C. shimming   D. joisting

21.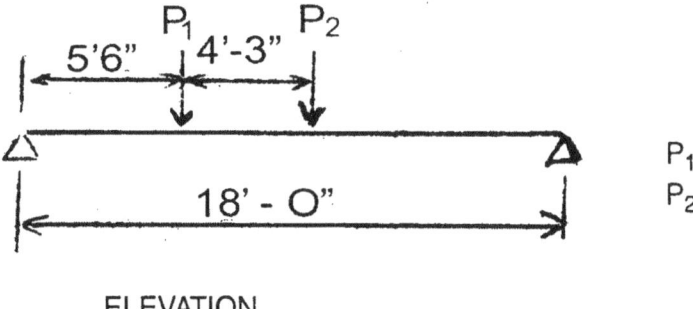

    $P_1 = 5,200$ #
    $P_2 = 4,300$ #

    ELEVATION

    The vertical shear, in pounds, one foot to the right of the concentrated load P_1, in the ELEVATION shown above, is MOST NEARLY

    A. 380   B. 520   C. 750   D. 930

22.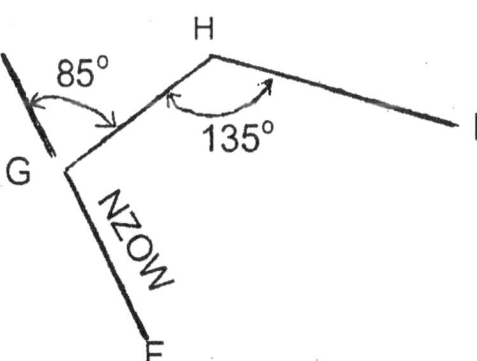

    In the layout shown on the preceding page, the bearing of line HI is

    A. N70E   B. N10W   C. S70E   D. N70W

23. A stairway with 7 treads needs _____ risers.

    A. 6 B. 7 C. 8 D. 9

24.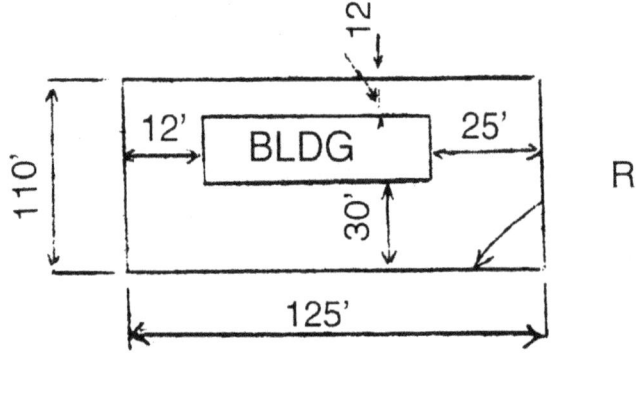

PLOT PLAN

In the above shown plot plan, the number of cubic yards of top soil, 6" deep, required to cover the tract is MOST NEARLY

    A. 115 B. 125 C. 135 D. 145

25. In structural steel work, it is usual practice NOT to paint surfaces that have been

    A. burned B. sheared C. milled D. coped

KEY (CORRECT ANSWERS)

1. D		11. B	
2. A		12. D	
3. C		13. B	
4. C		14. C	
5. A		15. B	
6. B		16. C	
7. A		17. A	
8. B		18. D	
9. D		19. C	
10. D		20. A	

21. A
22. C
23. C
24. D
25. C

TEST 2

DIRECTIONS: Each question or incomplete statement is followed by several suggested answers or completions. Select the one that BEST answers the question or completes the statement. *PRINT THE LETTER OF THE CORRECT ANSWER IN THE SPACE AT THE RIGHT.*

Questions 1-2.

DIRECTIONS: Questions 1 and 2 refer to the following sketch.

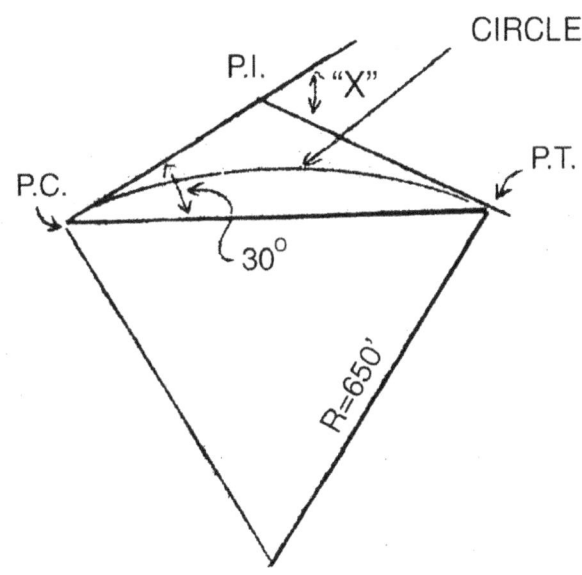

1. The angle X is

    A. 30°   B. 40°   C. 50°   D. 60°

2. The chord distance P.C. to P.T. is _____ feet.

    A. 225   B. 330   C. 650   D. 725

3. The is equal to MOST NEARLY

    A. 13.85   B. 13.90   C. 13.95   D. 14.00

4. A sounding with a lead line shows that the depth in the river is 29.8 feet. If the sounding is taken when the tide gage reads +3.4 feet above M.S.L. and the local datum is 1.9' above M.S.L., then the elevation of the bottom of the river with respect to the local datum is, in feet, MOST NEARLY

    A. -26.4   B. -28.3   C. -31.7   D. -35.1

51

5. The shaded area expressed algebraically is
   A. 4(X+Y/2)X
   B. $4(x^2+y^2)$
   C. (x+y)(x-y)
   D. 4(X+Y)X-2

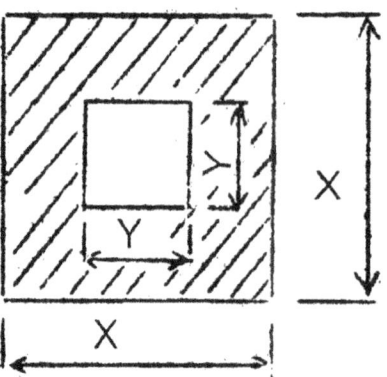

6. The valve that is placed before a fire hydrant in the city is a(n) _____ valve.
   A. angle   B. gate   C. check   D. globe

7. Of the following, the DENSEST liquid is
   A. oil   B. water   C. alcohol   D. mercury

8. The run-off, in C.F.S., from a tract 300 ft. x 830 ft., for a rainfall of 1.5 inches per hour and run-off 0.82 is MOST NEARLY (Q = C.i.A., when A is in acres. 1 acre = 43,560 sq.ft.)
   A. 4   B. 5   C. 6   D. 7

9. The resisting-moment, in foot kips, of the steel in a reinforced concrete beam whose A_s is 1.50, f_s is 24,000 p.s.i., j is 7/8, and effective depth 18 inches is MOST NEARLY ($M_s = A_s f_s jd$)
   A. 41   B. 43   C. 45   D. 47

10.

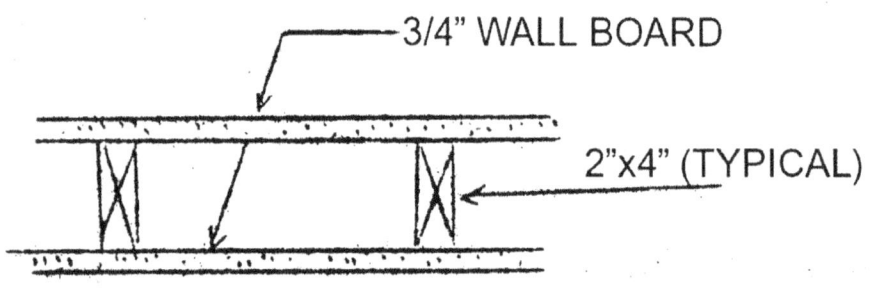

PLAN - PARTITION WALL

In the plan shown above, the 2" x 4" member is called a

A. joist   B. stud   C. cove   D. sheath

11. In the city, reinforcing steel is bent and placed by
    A. ornamental iron workers
    B. miscellaneous iron workers
    C. carpenters
    D. metal lathers

12. The white encrustation on the face of a wall caused by the presence of salts in the mortar or bricks is called

    A. amberescence
    B. deliquescense
    C. efflorescence
    D. echinuscense

13. A dam can be built *without* diverting the river by using

    A. corewalls
    B. cofferdams
    C. channels
    D. wallpoints

14. Of the following pipe materials, the one that is MOST commonly used to convey drinking water is

    A. clay
    B. wood
    C. cast iron
    D. polyethylene plastic

15. A gooseneck is MOST often required on a(n)

    A. steam line
    B. water service line
    C. sewer house connection
    D. electric house service

16. The x——x——x——x appearing on a topographical map represents a _____ line.

    A. fence   B. bulkhead   C. subway   D. water

17. In the sketch shown at the right, the horizontal molded projection at the top of the building is a
    A. camber
    B. cornice
    C. coping
    D. cant

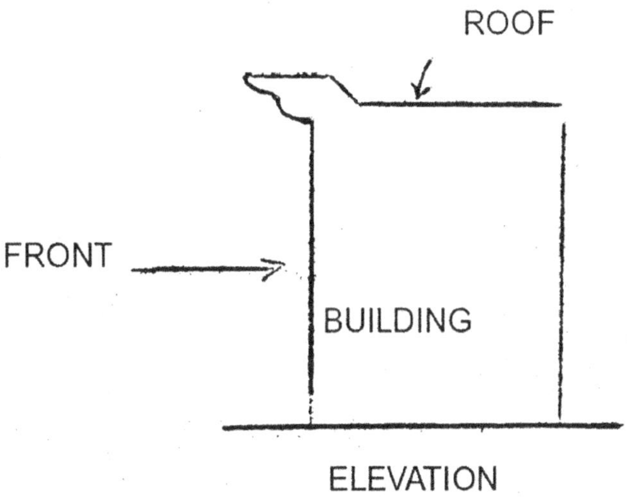

18. The moment of inertia, of the rectangle shown at the right, about the X-X axis is MOST NEARLY (I = 1/12bd^3)

    A. 162 ft^3
    B. 182.3 ft^3
    C. 364.5 ft^3
    D. 729 ft^3

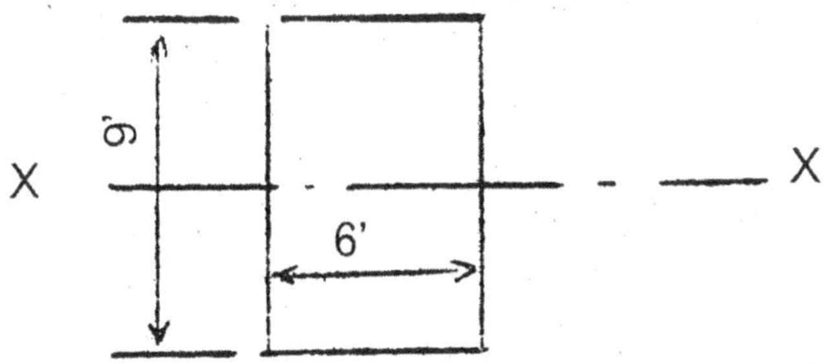

19. Galvanizing a steel surface USUALLY means coating it with

    A. cadmium   B. zinc   C. lead   D. tin

20. Of the following elements, the one that is LEAST active chemically is   20.____

    A. copper   B. lead   C. zinc   D. iron

21. The hydraulic radius of a circular pipe flowing full is   21.____

    A. r/2   B. 2/r   C. r/1   D. 1/r

22. The position in which the weld shown at the right is being made is   22.____
    A. side
    B. vertical
    C. flat
    D. horizontal

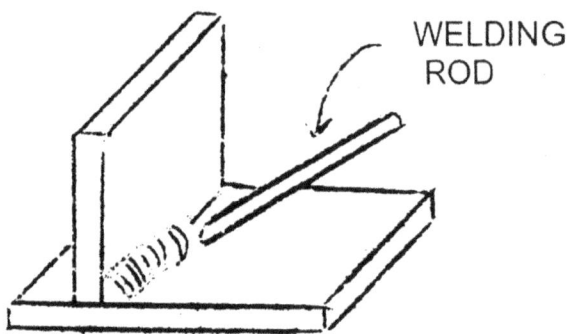

23. The figure shown at the right shows the results of a survey made with a 100.00 ft. steel tape. The tape was later standardized and found to be 99.97 feet long. The CORRECT perimeter, in feet, based on the true length of the tape is MOST NEARLY   23.____
    A. 2466.97
    B. 2467.04
    C. 2467.50
    D. 2468.57

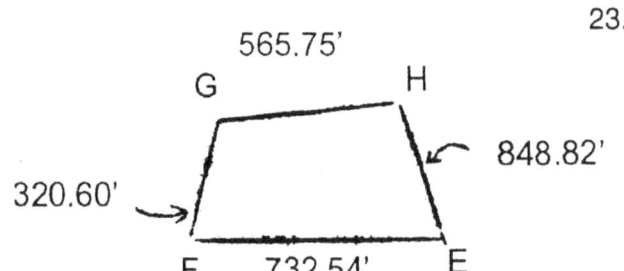

24. Of the following elements, the one that is PREDOMINANT in structural is   24.____

    A. S   B. F_e C. S_i D. M_n

25.   25.____

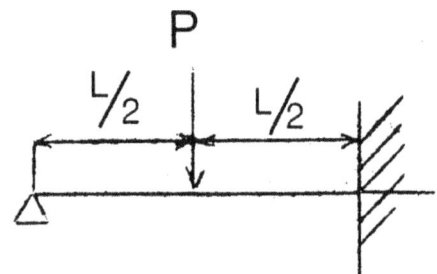

For the beam loading shown above, the shear diagram should look MOST NEARLY like

5 (#2)

A.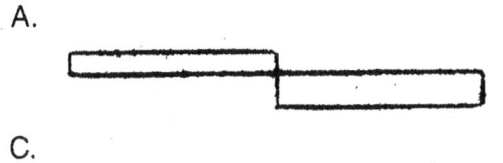

B.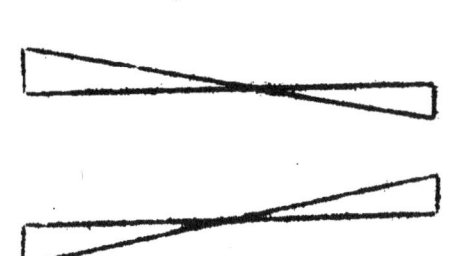

C.

D.

KEY (CORRECT ANSWERS)

1.	D		11.	D
2.	C		12.	C
3.	B		13.	B
4.	B		14.	C
5.	C		15.	B
6.	B		16.	A
7.	D		17.	B
8.	D		18.	C
9.	D		19.	B
10.	B		20.	B

21. A
22. D
23. A
24. B
25. A

TEST 3

DIRECTIONS: Each question or incomplete statement is followed by several suggested answers or completions. Select the one that BEST answers the question or completes the statement. *PRINT THE LETTER OF THE CORRECT ANSWER IN THE SPACE AT THE RIGHT.*

Questions 1-2.

DIRECTIONS: Questions 1 and 2 refer to the vertical curve shown below.

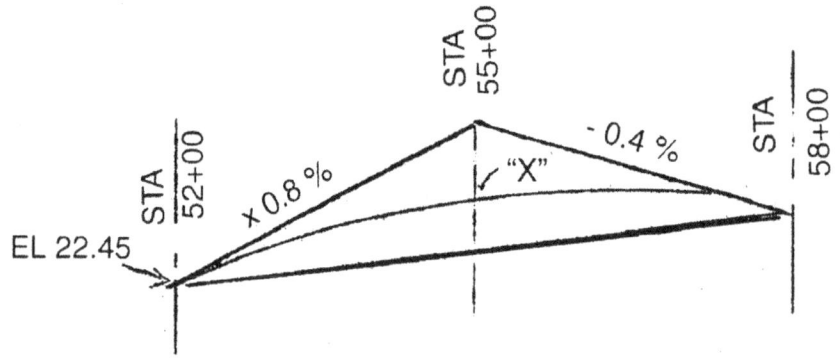

1. The algebraic difference in gradient between the two slopes is

   A. 0.6%   B. -0.8%   C. +1.0%   D. +1.2%

   1._____

2. The elevation of point X on the curve is

   A. 22.80'   B. 23.25'   C. 23.55'   D. 23.95'

   2._____

3. Plain concrete is USUALLY composed of

   A. cement, sand, and gravel
   B. cement and sand
   C. cement, crushed rock, and gravel
   D. gypsum and sand

   3._____

4. If a 100-feet-long steel tape expands 5/64" for a temperature rise of 10°F, then the expansion of a 91-feet-long steel tape with a temperature rise of 70°F is

   A. 3/8"   B. 1/2"   C. 3/4"   D. 7/8"

   4._____

5. Of the following, the one that is NOT used as a lightweight aggregate for concrete is

   A. cinders   B. traprock
   C. pumice   D. vermiculite

   5._____

6. In tunnel construction, the points that mark the center line of the tunnel are USUALLY set

   A. in the roof of the tunnel
   B. on the ground four feet off the center line of the tunnel
   C. on the ground at the center line of the tunnel
   D. on the side of the tunnel at center line elevation

   6._____

7. The high rod reading shown at the right is
   A. 8.100
   B. 8.125
   C. 8.135
   D. 8.250

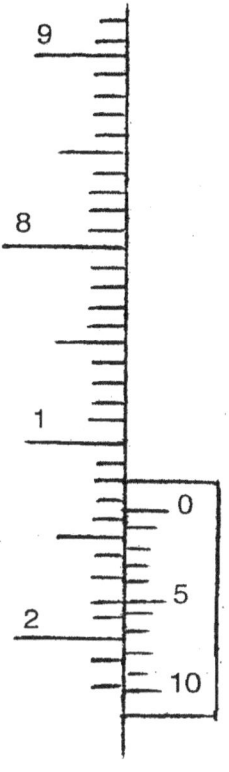

8. The value of 6!/72 is
   A. 10   B. 12   C. 14   D. 16

9. The fourth term of the binomial $(X+a)^5$ is
   A. $15a^4X^3$ B. $10a^3X^2$ C. a^5 D. $5aX^4$

10. If steel weighs 490 #/cu.ft., then the cross-sectional area, in square inches, of an 8[11.5 is MOST NEARLY
    A. 3.04   B. 3.22   C. 3.38   D. 3.45

11.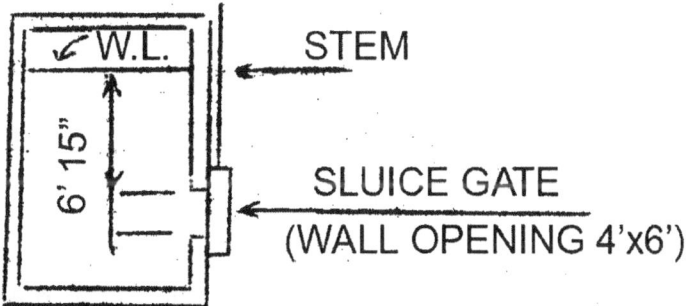

    The total horizontal water pressure, in pounds, acting on the above shown sluice gate is MOST NEARLY
    A. 23,000   B. 25,000   C. 27,000   D. 29,000

12. Terrazzo would MOST likely be found on
    A. ceilings   B. floors
    C. interior walls   D. exterior walls

13. In the laying out of a building foundation, batter boards are set

    A. outside the corners of the building
    B. inside the sides of the building
    C. inside diagonally opposite corners of the building only
    D. outside one side and inside one corner of the building only

    13._____

14. The value of the determinant shown at the right is

    $\begin{vmatrix} 8 & 5 \\ 2 & 1 \end{vmatrix}$

    A. 37
    B. 16
    C. 10
    D. -2

    14._____

15. If the product of the slopes of two lines is -1, then the lines are

    A. 30° to each other
    B. perpendicular
    C. parallel
    D. collinear

    15._____

16. Blowoffs are provided on water mains to

    A. provide access to inspect the main
    B. remove sediment in the lines
    C. prevent the buildup of excessive pressure
    D. minimize the effect of water hammer

    16._____

17. A 10-foot section of a 48" round sewer settles 6 inches.
    Of the following, the MOST probable consequence of this condition is the

    A. reduction in the carrying capacity of the pipe
    B. possibility of an air lock at this point
    C. stoppage of flow due to sediment
    D. possibility of cavitation in the pipe

    17._____

18. The clearance of bridges over navigable waterways is the *official* concern of the

    A. Coast and Geodetic Survey
    B. Navy Department
    C. U.S. Army
    D. Department of the Interior

    18._____

19. On a highway project, a test that is USUALLY performed to determine the compaction of the subbase is a _____ test.

    A. density
    B. slump
    C. compression
    D. grain size

    19._____

20. Of the following, the statement that is CORRECT with respect to transverse joints in pavements is:
    A(n)

    A. expansion joint allows for both expansion and contraction
    B. contraction joint allows for both expansion and contraction
    C. warping joint allows for both expansion and contraction
    D. warping joint allows for both contraction and warping

    20._____

21. The curve that facilitates the transition from the normal crowned straight section of a roadway to the banked curved section of roadway is known as a(n)

    A. spiral easement
    B. parabola
    C. simple circle
    D. hyperbola

22. In trench excavation, a pair of vertical boards placed on opposite sides of a trench with two cross braces holding then is known as

    A. vertical sheeting
    B. poling boards
    C. box sheeting
    D. stay bracing

23. The penetration test on asphalt cement is used to determine its

    A. density
    B. hardness
    C. elasticity
    D. time of set

24. A concrete column with an effective cross-section 20 inches square has one percent vertical steel reinforcing with proper ties.
    Assuming fc = 500 pounds per square inch and n = 15, the capacity of the column for taking axial load, in pounds, is APPROXIMATELY (P = fc[1+(n-1)Po])

    A. 175,000
    B. 200,000
    C. 225,000
    D. 250,000

25. Turning of metals is USUALLY performed on a

    A. radial drill press
    B. lathe
    C. milling machine
    D. shaper

KEY (CORRECT ANSWERS)

1.	D	11.	C
2.	D	12.	B
3.	A	13.	A
4.	B	14.	D
5.	B	15.	B
6.	A	16.	B
7.	C	17.	A
8.	A	18.	C
9.	B	19.	A
10.	C	20.	A

21. A
22. D
23. B
24. C
25. B

TEST 4

DIRECTIONS: Each question or incomplete statement is followed by several suggested answers or completions. Select the one that BEST answers the question or completes the statement. *PRINT THE LETTER OF THE CORRECT ANSWER IN THE SPACE AT THE RIGHT.*

1. An eighth of an inch is equal MOST NEARLY to _____ of a foot.   1._____
   A. 1/10   B. 1/100   C. 1/64   D. 1/84

2.   2._____

   In the sketch above, the type of internal stress acting on the member along line A-A due to the load P shown above is

   A. tension and compression *only*
   B. tension and shear *only*
   C. tension, compression, and shear
   D. shear *only*

3. Lime used in mortar is USUALLY   3._____
   A. hydrated lime   B. quicklime
   C. unslaked lime   D. plaster of paris

4. An air entraining compound is PRIMARILY added to concrete to   4._____
   A. make it light
   B. make it set early
   C. eliminate the need for curing
   D. make it more durable

5. The arrangement of bricks shown at the right is _____ Bond.   5._____
   A. English
   B. Flemish
   C. Common
   D. Danish

6. The coverage of a paint is 360 sq.ft./gallon. The number of gallons required to paint the walls of four rooris, 11'1" x 12'8" by 7'6" high, with one coat, is MOST NEARLY (do not count windows or doors)   6._____
   A. 2   B. 3   C. 4   D. 5

7. In the ELEVATION shown at the right, stone X is known as a
   A. reglet
   B. baffle
   C. perron
   D. coping

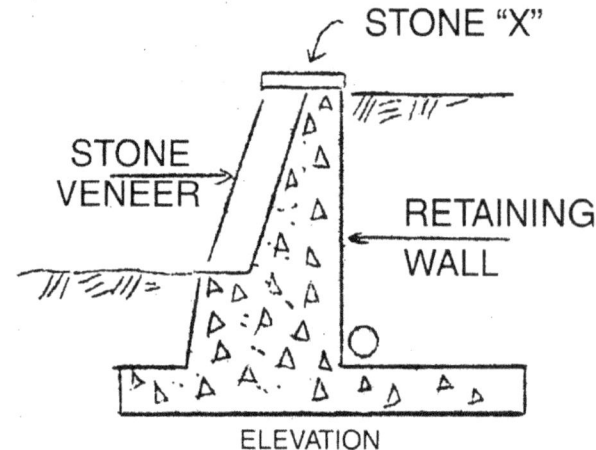

8. The material MOST commonly used as a conductor in ordinary electric wiring is
   A. brass   B. zinc   C. copper   D. aluminum

9. In trigonometry, the expression Cos X cos Y - Sin X sin Y
   A. Sin(X+Y)   B. Sin(X-Y)   C. Cos(X+Y)   D. Cos(X-Y)

10. In the window shown at the right, X is called a
    A. jamb
    B. muntin
    C. stool
    D. mullion

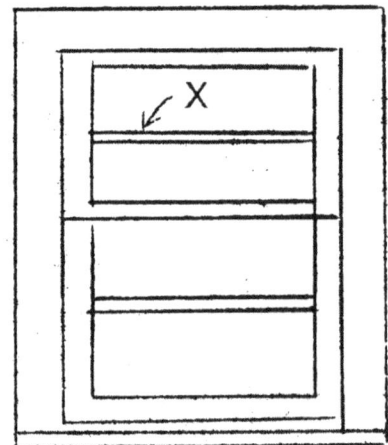

11. If the Sin X = .60, then the Cos X =
    A. .50   B. .60   C. .70   D. .80

12. The length of a meter is, in inches, MOST NEARLY
    A. 39.4   B. 38.6   C. 37.2   D. 36.9

13. To complete the square in the terms $X^2 + 10X$, we would have to add
    A. 20   B. 25   C. 30   D. 100

14. In the sketch shown at the right, the distance X - Y is MOST NEARLY
    A. 8'5"
    B. 8'8"
    C. 9'0"
    D. 9'3"

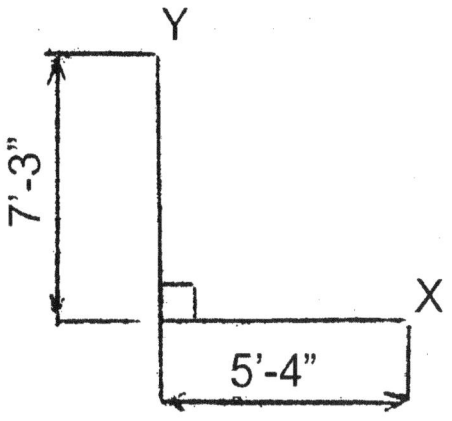

15. A rectangular footing is to have an area of 250 square feet. If the length is to be twice its width, then the width is MOST NEARLY

    A. 11.0'   B. 11.2'   C. 11.4'   D. 11.5'

16. In the term *4000 pound concrete*, the term *4000 pound,* as applied to ordinary concrete, represents the ultimate compressive strength of the concrete at the end of _____ days.

    A. 3   B. 7   C. 14   D. 28

17.

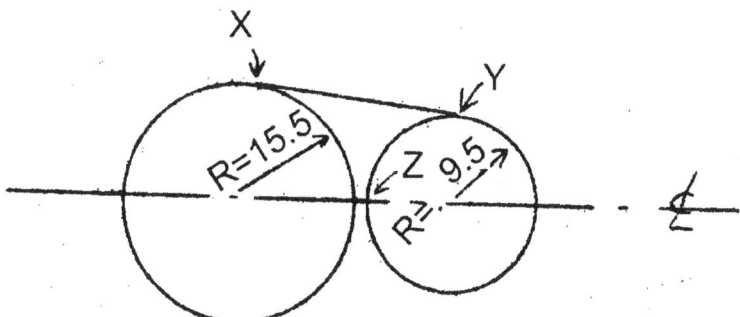

In the sketch shown above, the length of the common tangent XY to the two circles tangent at Z is

    A. 21.3   B. 22.3   C. 23.3   D. 24.3

18. Sin(X+90)° is equal to

    A. Cos X   B. Sin X   C. - Cos X   D. - Sin X

19. In a contract that includes both unit-price and lump-sum items, the one that is LEAST likely to be bid on a unit-price basis is

    A. cleaning up   B. seeding and mulching
    C. fencing   D. waterstops

20. The PRIMARY reason for providing sewers with manholes is to
    A. ventilate the sewage
    B. clean and inspect the sewer
    C. connect future house connections
    D. allow sewer to surcharge

21. The number of radians in the arc of a circle having a central angle of 30° is 21.____

   A. $\pi/6$ B. $\pi/5$ C. $\pi/4$ D. $\pi/3$

22. The weight of a cubic foot of cement is, in pounds, MOST NEARLY 22.____

   A. 86   B. 90   C. 94   D. 98

23. The invert elevation at a manhole of a sewer is 65.40'. If the slope of the pipe is .0063 ft./ ft., then the invert elevation at a manhole 275 ft. downstream is 23.____

   A. 63.25'   B. 63.67'   C. 63.85'   D. 63.98'

24. The cutting out of the top flange and web of a steel member so that the steel member will frame into another steel member is called 24.____

   A. coping   B. crimping   C. canting   D. corbelling

25. The architectural symbol [∩∪∩∪] is a section representing 25.____

   A. marble
   C. clay tile
   B. glazed tile
   D. insulation

KEY (CORRECT ANSWERS)

1.	B	11.	D
2.	C	12.	A
3.	A	13.	B
4.	D	14.	C
5.	B	15.	B
6.	C	16.	D
7.	D	17.	D
8.	C	18.	A
9.	C	19.	A
10.	B	20.	B

21. A
22. C
23. B
24. A
25. D

EXAMINATION SECTION
TEST 1

DIRECTIONS: Each question or incomplete statement is followed by several suggested answers or completions. Select the one that BEST answers the question or completes the statement. *PRINT THE LETTER OF THE CORRECT ANSWER IN THE SPACE AT THE RIGHT.*

1. Assume that a two story building measures 21'6" x 53'7". It is in a district that calls for an open space ratio of .80. The required open space on this lot must be *most nearly* square feet. 1.____

   A. 922 B. 1152 C. 1843 D. 2880

2. Assume that the elevation at the back of a lot is 127.36 ft. and the elevation at the front of the same lot is 125.49 ft. 2.____
   The difference in elevation between front and back of the lot is *most nearly*

   A. 1'10 1/8" B. 1'10 1/4" C. 1'10 3/8" D. 1'10 1/2"

3. The sketch below represents the lowest story of a new building. In order for this story to be considered a basement, the elevation of the first floor must be AT LEAST 3.____

   A. 131.09 B. 131.14 C. 131.19 D. 131.24

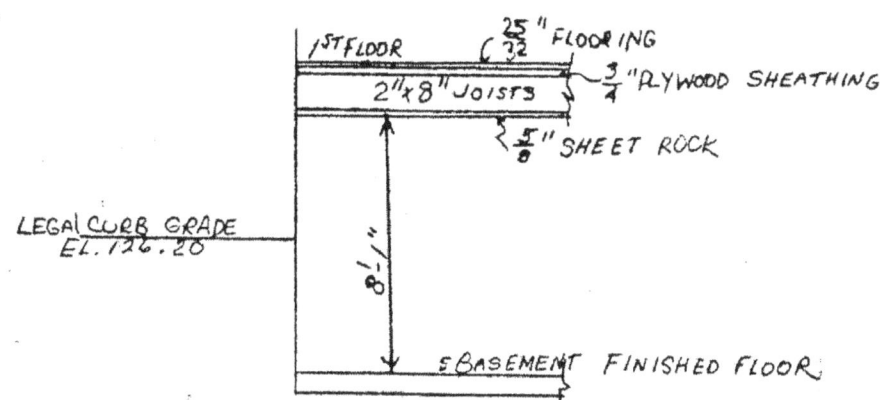

4. The MOST important requirement of a good report is that it should be 4.____

   A. properly addressed B. clear and concise
   C. verbose D. spelled correctly

5. Of the following, in determining whether a violation should be referred for court action, the MOST important item that should be considered is 5.____

   A. the amount of available time you have to process the case
   B. the availability of the inspector
   C. whether or not the owner has indicated a desire to cooperate with the department
   D. whether or not the case is important enough to warrant court action

6. In the Zoning Resolution, the size of required side yards would be found in the chapters on

   A. Use Groups
   B. Bulk Regulations
   C. Area Districts
   D. District Boundaries

7. According to the Zoning Resolution, the one of the following that is NOT considered part of the floor area of a building is a(n)

   A. basement
   B. stairwell at floor level
   C. penthouse
   D. attached garage on 1st floor

8. The one of the following that is permitted by the Zoning Resolution as a home occupation is

   A. veterinary medicine
   B. real estate broker
   C. teaching of music
   D. public relations agency

9. For the purpose of determining the number of rooms in a dwelling unit, the Zoning Resolution adds an arbitrary number to the number of *living rooms*.
   Where there are six or less living rooms, this arbitrary number is

   A. 1/2   B. 1   C. 1 1/2   D. 2

10. Assuming the following signs are all 10 square feet in area, the one that is NOT subject to the provisions of the Zoning Resolution is one indicating

    A. a freight entrance to a building
    B. a fund drive for a civic organization
    C. vacancies in an apartment building
    D. a parking area at the rear of a structure

11. On a plan, the symbol represents

    A. earth
    B. wood
    C. metal lath
    D. marble

12. On a plan, the symbol represents

    A. cinder
    B. brick
    C. plywood
    D. rock lath and plaster

13. On a plan, the symbol represents

    A. glass
    B. asphalt shingles
    C. concrete
    D. porcelain enamel

14. A corbel is a form of   14._____

    A. cricket B. crown molding
    C. cantilever D. curtain wall

15. In balloon type framing, the second floor joists rest on a   15._____

    A. sole plate B. ribband
    C. header D. sill

16. Condensation of moisture in inadequately ventilated attics or roof spaces is usually GREATEST in   16._____

    A. summer B. autumn C. winter D. spring

17. Of the following combinations of tread and riser, the one that would be acceptable for required stairs in either a new office building or a multiple dwelling is   17._____

    A. 9 1/4", 7 1/2" B. 9 1/2", 7 1/4"
    C. 9 1/2", 7 3/4" D. 10", 8"

18. A meeting rail is a common part of a   18._____

    A. door frame B. window sash
    C. stairwell D. bulkhead

19. If doors in an old building do not close, it is MOST probably an indication that the   19._____

    A. frames have shrunk
    B. building has settled
    C. hinges were not set properly
    D. wood used for the doors are of inferior grade

20. Cracks in concrete are not necessarily caused by settlement of a structure. Sometimes they are caused by   20._____

    A. shrinkage B. curing
    C. hydration D. over-troweling

KEY (CORRECT ANSWERS)

1.	C	11.	A
2.	D	12.	B
3.	A	13.	A
4.	B	14.	C
5.	C	15.	B
6.	B	16.	C
7.	D	17.	C
8.	C	18.	B
9.	C	19.	B
10.	B	20.	A

TEST 2

DIRECTIONS: Each question or incomplete statement is followed by several suggested answers or completions. Select the one that BEST answers the question or completes the statement. *PRINT THE LETTER OF THE CORRECT ANSWER IN THE SPACE AT THE RIGHT.*

1. Required exit doors from a room must open in the direction of egress when the room is occupied by more than _____ persons.

    A. 15　　B. 25　　C. 35　　D. 50

2. A window in a masonry wall on a lot line

    A. is not permitted
    B. must have a fire resistive rating of 3/4 hour
    C. must have a fire resistive rating of 1 hour
    D. must have a fire resistive rating of 1 1/2 hours

3. Air entrained concrete is required in all cases for

    A. garage floors　　B. footings
    C. grade beams　　D. columns

4. A parapet wall or railing would be required on new non-residential structures where the height of the structure is greater than (give lowest height specified by law) _____ feet.

    A. 15　　B. 19　　C. 22　　D. 25

5. Of the following statements, the one that is CORRECT is that wood joists may

    A. not be supported on a fire wall
    B. be supported on a fire wall only if fireproofed wall is used
    C. be supported on a fire wall only if they are separated from each other by at least 4 inches of solid masonry
    D. be supported on a fire wall only if they are separated from each other by at least 12 inches of solid masonry

6. A foundation wall below grade may be of hollow block only if the building

    A. is a residence
    B. is no more than one story high
    C. is of frame construction
    D. has no cellar or basement

7. The Building Code specifies that lintels are required to be fire-proofed when the opening is more than _____ feet.

    A. 3　　B. 4　　C. 5　　D. 6

8. In a 12-inch brick wall, the MAXIMUM permitted depth of a chase is

    A. none　　B. 4"　　C. 6"　　D. 8"

9. Wood joists should clear flues and chimneys by at least

    A. 1"　　B. 2"　　C. 3"　　D. 4"

10. Fire retarding or enclosure in shafts of all vent ducts are required when they   10._____

    A. go through more than one floor
    B. are used for intake as well as exhaust
    C. are more than 144 square inches in area
    D. are in rooms subdivided with wood partitions

11. Assume a builder is unable to complete the pour for a continuous concrete floor slab. The   11._____
    slab is supported by beams and girders.
    The construction joint should be made at a point

    A. over a beam
    B. one quarter of the span length from the beam
    C. one third of the span length from the beam
    D. midway between beams

12. Under required stairs in a Class 3 building,   12._____

    A. it is unlawful to locate a closet
    B. a closet is permitted provided that the stringers are fire retarded
    C. a closet is permitted provided that the closet is completely lined with incombustible material
    D. a closet is permitted provided that fireproof wood is used to frame out the closet

13. In New York City, the exit provisions of the State Labor Law apply   13._____

    A. only to factories
    B. to factories and warehouses
    C. to factories, warehouses, and restaurants
    D. to all types of uses

14. A Class 3 building, two stories high, may have required stairs enclosed with stud parti-   14._____
    tions fire retarded with gypsum boards unless the building is used for a

    A. factory   B. storage warehouse
    C. bowling alley   D. department store

15. The one of the following rooms in a *place of assembly* that is required to be sprinklered is   15._____
    a

    A. performer's dressing room
    B. kitchen
    C. service pantry
    D. waiting room

16. Of the following, the FIRST operation in the demolition of a building is the   16._____

    A. shoring of the adjoining buildings
    B. erection of railings around stairwells
    C. removal of windows
    D. venting of the roof

17. As used in the Building Code, *consistency* of concrete refers to   17._____

    A. composition   B. water-cement ratio
    C. relative plasticity   D. proportion of aggregates

18. One condition that is required for a building to be considered a *Special Occupancy Structure* is that the building is used for

    A. a theater
    B. a church
    C. a restaurant
    D. motor vehicle repairs

19. A wire glass vision panel on a door opening into a fire tower is

    A. not permitted
    B. permitted if the panel has a fire rating of 3/4 hour
    C. permitted if the panel has a fire rating of 3/4 hour and is less than 100 square inches in area
    D. permitted if the panel has a fire rating of 3/4 hour, is less than 100 square inches in area, and is glazed with two thicknesses of wire glass with an air space between

20. One of the requirements that must be met before untreated wood can be used as a subdividing partition in a Class 1 building is that the partition

    A. be no more than 8 feet high
    B. enclose an area less than 200 square feet in size
    C. enclose office space only
    D. be made of a single thickness of wood

KEY (CORRECT ANSWERS)

1.	D	11.	D
2.	B	12.	C
3.	A	13.	A
4.	C	14.	C
5.	C	15.	A
6.	D	16.	C
7.	B	17.	C
8.	B	18.	A
9.	D	19.	A
10.	A	20.	D

TEST 3

DIRECTIONS: Each question or incomplete statement is followed by several suggested answers or completions. Select the one that BEST answers the question or completes the statement. *PRINT THE LETTER OF THE CORRECT ANSWER IN THE SPACE AT THE RIGHT.*

1. There are two criteria required for determining whether a multiple dwelling shall be classified as a *converted dwelling*.
   The FIRST is the number of families originally occupying the dwelling, and the second is the

   A. conjunctive uses
   B. date of erection of the building
   C. classification, whether Class A or B
   D. number of families now occupying the dwelling

   1.____

2. According to the Multiple Dwelling Law, a *dinette* is NOT considered a living room if its area is _____ sq. ft. or less.

   A. 50 B. 55 C. 59 D. 64

   2.____

3. Where a building faces only one street, the curb level used for measuring the height of the building is the

   A. lowest curb level in front of the building
   B. highest curb level in front of the building
   C. level of the curb at the center of the front of the building
   D. average of the levels of the lowest and highest curb level in front of the building

   3.____

4. According to the Multiple Dwelling Code, one of the living rooms in each apartment of a newly created multiple dwelling shall have a MINIMUM floor area of _____ square feet.

   A. 59 B. 110 C. 150 D. 175

   4.____

5. It is proposed to alter an old law tenement so as to increase the number of apartments. Of the following, the one that MOST completely gives the requirements to be met before the alteration can be approved is: Each new apartment must be provided a

   A. water closet
   B. water closet and a wash basin
   C. water closet, a wash basin, and a bath or shower
   D. water closet, a wash basin, a bath or shower, and centrally supplied heat

   5.____

6. Gas fueled space heaters may be permitted in lieu of centrally supplied heat.
   One of the following conditions required before the use of space heaters can be permitted is that

   A. each apartment has no more than two living rooms
   B. the building is a Class A multiple dwelling
   C. all apartments are used for single room occupancy
   D. D, the gas line supplying the heater be connected directly to the main so that the tenant cannot control the flow of gas

   6.____

7. An incinerator is required in all multiple

   A. dwellings
   B. dwellings four or more stories in height
   C. dwellings four or more stories in height and occupied by more than twelve families
   D. dwellings four or more stories in height occupied by more than twelve families and erected after October 1, 1951

8. Tests of required sprinkler systems in a single room occupancy building must be made

   A. monthly
   B. quarterly
   C. semi-annually
   D. annually

9. An additional apartment may be created on the first floor of a Class A frame converted dwelling provided that no more than two families will occupy this floor and

   A. the entrance hall is sprinklered
   B. the building is brick veneered
   C. there is no basement occupancy
   D. all stairs are enclosed in one hour fire partitions

10. The MAIN feature differentiating a *five tower* from a *fire stair* is the

    A. fire rating of the enclosure walls
    B. use to which the fire tower is put
    C. method of entering the fire tower from the building
    D. height of the fire tower

11. A new elevator shaft is to be built into a non-fireproof multiple dwelling.
    Of the following materials, the one that has the lowest fire resistance that would be acceptable for the enclosure walls of this shaft is

    A. 3" solid gypsum block
    B. 2" x 4" studs with 5/8" fire code 60 each side
    C. steel studs, wire mesh and 3/4" P.C. plaster
    D. 4" hollow concrete blocks, plastered both sides

12. Of the following statements, the one that is MOST complete and accurate is that a frame extension 70 sq. ft. in area added to a frame multiple dwelling is

    A. not permitted
    B. permitted only if the walls of the extension are brick filled
    C. permitted only if the walls of the extension are brick filled and the extension is to be used solely for bathrooms
    D. permitted only if the walls of the extension are brick filled, the extension is to be used solely for bathrooms and the walls are at least 3 ft. from the side lot lines

13. Assume it is proposed to extend a business use in a non-fireproof multiple dwelling by erecting an extension at the rear of the building.
    The roof the extension is required to be fireproof

    A. in all cases
    B. when the business use requires a combustible occupancy permit
    C. when there are fire escapes above the extension
    D. if the business use is a factory

14. In a Class A dwelling, two water closets may

    A. be placed in one compartment only in old law tenements
    B. be placed in one compartment in either old law or new law tenements
    C. be placed in one compartment in all types of apartment houses
    D. not be placed in one compartment

14.____

15. According to the Multiple Dwelling Law, a janitor is NOT required when the maximum number of families occupying the dwelling is

    A. 6 B. 9 C. 12 D. 15

15.____

16. The first floor above the lowest cellar in a non-fireproof multiple dwelling does NOT have to be fireproof if

    A. the cellar is used only for incombustible storage
    B. there are two means of egress from the cellar
    C. the building is no more than three stories in height
    D. the dwelling is occupied by no more than nine families

16.____

17. In a converted multiple dwelling, ventilation of a room on the top story may be obtained by

    A. a skylight
    B. a duct with a wind blown hood
    C. a duct with an electrically operated fan
    D. by a window only and no other method is acceptable

17.____

18. It is proposed to build a closet under the stairs leading to the second floor in a non-fireproof *new law* tenement. This is

    A. not permitted
    B. permitted only if the entire closet is built of non-combustible materials
    C. permitted only if the closet is used for non-combustible storage
    D. permitted if the closet is built of fire-retarded partitions and the soffit of the stairs is also fire-retarded

18.____

19. For multiple dwellings erected after April 18, 1929, a ladder from a fire escape to a roof is NOT required when

    A. the building is three stories or less in height
    B. the roof is built of incombustible material
    C. the fire escape is on the front of the building
    D. there is no safe access from the roof to another building

19.____

20. It is proposed to convert a Class B multiple dwelling used for summer resort occupancy to year-round Class B use. This conversion is

    A. illegal
    B. legal provided the exits comply with the requirements for Class B use
    C. legal provided the exits and toilet facilities comply with the requirements for Class B use
    D. legal provided the exits, toilet facilities, and ventilation requirements comply with the requirements for Class B use

20.____

KEY (CORRECT ANSWERS)

1. B
2. B
3. C
4. C
5. D

6. B
7. D
8. D
9. B
10. C

11. A
12. A
13. C
14. A
15. C

16. C
17. A
18. A
19. C
20. A

EXAMINATION SECTION
TEST 1

DIRECTIONS: Each question or incomplete statement is followed by several suggested answers or completions. Select the one that BEST answers the question or completes the statement. *PRINT THE LETTER OF THE CORRECT ANSWER IN THE SPACE AT THE RIGHT.*

1. When a sidewalk shed is required in connection with the erection of a building, the Code provides that the shed must be completed before the building has risen to a height, in feet, of

    A. 12   B. 16   C. 30   D. 40

2. Concrete for a self-supporting floor should have a slump, in inches, of about

    A. 3   B. 4   C. 7   D. 13

3. When building material bears a distinguishing mark of the manufacturer, the inspector should

    A. ignore it
    B. ask the contractor to remove it
    C. check to see if the mark is approved by the Board
    D. ask the contractor to obtain the manufacturer's specifications

4. The letters *A.S.T.M.* followed by letters and numbers refer to

    A. standard tests of materials
    B. paragraphs in state laws
    C. sections, text, and meaning of the Building Code
    D. the structural training manual

5. A frame building with 2 x 4 studding has an interior partition with 2 x 6 studding. The MOST probable reason for the heavier studding is to provide

    A. heat insulation
    B. sound insulation
    C. room for a soil stack
    D. room for steam pipes

6. Ties and chairs are used in construction involving

    A. plain concrete
    B. reinforced concrete
    C. masonry
    D. structural steel

7. Painting of steel reinforcing bars is

    A. *bad*, because it impairs bond
    B. *good*, because it prevents rust
    C. *bad*, because it increases costs
    D. *good*, because use of different colors permits ready identification of the various sizes

8. An inspector picks up a brick, which has just been laid, to inspect the bedding. No mortar adhered to the brick so the furrowing of the mortar is shown clearly.
The inspector is MOST concerned with the

   A. depth of the furrow
   B. width of the furrow
   C. depth and width of the furrow
   D. fact that no mortar adhered to the brick

9. Acoustic tile would MOST likely be used in

   A. ceilings   B. floors   C. bathrooms   D. kitchens

10. To determine the story heights of a building, you should look at the

    A. plan view
    B. elevation view
    C. architect's rendition
    D. perspective view

11. Kalamein work is

    A. metal-sheathed wood
    B. a type of enameling
    C. woodwork using different colored woods to make a pattern
    D. used in ornamental plastering

12. The weight of all permanent construction in a building is known as _____ load.

    A. permanent   B. live   C. dead   D. design

13. A layer of plaster which is scratched both horizontally and vertically is known as a

    A. scratch coat
    B. bond coat
    C. brown coat
    D. plaster base

14. When steel is given two coats of paint, a different color is used for the second coat

    A. for a pleasing contrast
    B. to avoid monotony for the painter
    C. for chemical reasons
    D. to insure full coverage by the second coat

15. A certificate of occupancy is required for a new building

    A. if it is a Class A multiple dwelling
    B. if it is a multiple dwelling
    C. if it is a dwelling
    D. regardless of whether or not it is a dwelling

16. New multiple dwelling of non-fireproof construction

    A. is not allowed
    B. must be outside the fire limits
    C. must not exceed 75 feet in height
    D. must not occupy more than 70% of the lot area

17. In an elevation view, round reinforcing bars in a reinforced concrete floor would appear as

    A. circles
    B. lines
    C. either circles or line
    D. triangles

18. The columns of a building are spaced 21'0" in one direction and 28'0" in the other. The length of a diagonal of a bay is, in feet, MOST NEARLY

    A. 35.0   B. 35.1   C. 36.2   D. 34.9

19. The use of peaveys or cant hooks to handle creosoted lumber in wood construction is

    A. *bad,* because it may expose untreated wood
    B. *good,* because the laborer will not get splinters in his hands
    C. *bad,* because the lumber is damaged by rolling
    D. *good,* because it is an efficient method

20. The end of a joist resting on a masonry wall is USUALLY cut on a bevel to

    A. prevent damage to the wall if the joist should fall during a fire
    B. provide circulation of air around the enclosed portion of the joist
    C. provide a larger bearing area
    D. reduce the wall opening required by the joist

21. Oiling of steel reinforcing bars for concrete is

    A. *good,* because it prevents rust
    B. *good,* because it makes handling in the forms easier
    C. *bad,* because there is a chemical reaction with the concrete
    D. *bad,* because it prevents adhesion of the concrete

22. A load-bearing cavity wall consists of a four inch wythe and an eight inch wythe with a two inch air space.
    In normal construction, the wider wythe

    A. should be the outer face of the wall
    B. should be the inner face of the wall
    C. may be either inner or outer face
    D. wastes material as the two wythes should be of equal thickness

23. Metal ties used in cavity walls sometimes have a crimp which is located in the air space when the tie is in place in the wall.
    This crimp serves to

    A. strengthen the tie
    B. add to the elasticity of the tie
    C. prevent water from traveling across the tie
    D. center the tie between the wythes

Questions 24-25.

DIRECTIONS: Questions 24 and 25 refer to the following statement and sketch.

A specification reads: *Net cross-sectional area of a masonry unit shall be taken as the gross cross-sectional area minus the area of cores or cellular space.*

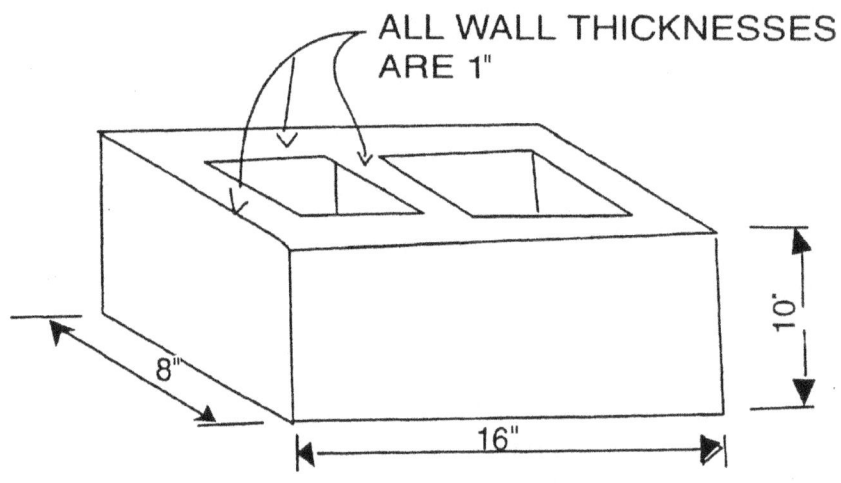

24. The gross cross-sectional area is _____ square inches.

    A. 64   B. 84   C. 128   D. 144

25. The net cross-sectional area is _____ square inches.

    A. 128   B. 112   C. 77   D. 50

26. Small wood members which are inserted in a diagonal position between floor joists for the purpose of bracing the joists and spreading loads to adjacent joists are called

    A. struts   B. ties   C. bridging   D. ledger strips

27. A beam placed perpendicular to joists and to which joists are nailed in framing for a chimney, stairway, or other opening, is called a

    A. trimmer joist   B. tail beam
    C. girder   D. header

28. A narrow board let into the studding to provide added support for joists is known as a

    A. sill   B. trimmer   C. ribbon   D. sole plate

29. In concrete construction, honeycombing is MOST likely to occur in

    A. thin floors   B. thin walls
    C. heavy footing   D. thick floors

30. The CHIEF objection to the use of green lumber in wood construction relates to its

    A. color
    B. strength
    C. lack of dimensional stability
    D. nailing

31. Concrete weighs 4000 pounds per cubic yard.
    A slab of concrete 4'3" wide by 7'6" long by 1'9" thick weighs, in pounds, MOST NEARLY

    A. 7550   B. 7950   C. 8000   D. 8260

32. A fire-resistive rating of an assembly is given in units of

    A. degrees centigrade
    B. degrees fahrenheit
    C. hours
    D. none of the above

33. A trimmer arch would be used in

    A. floor openings
    B. wall openings
    C. floor construction near chimneys
    D. parapet walls

34. Cracks in lumber due to contraction along annual rings are known as

    A. checks   B. pitch pockets   C. wane   D. craze

35. The length of a tenpenny nail, in inches, is

    A. 2 1/2   B. 3   C. 3 1/2   D. 4

36. When ready-mix concrete is used on a job, the PRIMARY responsibility for checking the proportioning of cement, sand, and gravel rests with

    A. the inspector on the job
    B. the engineer on the job
    C. the inspector at the batching plant
    D. none of the above

37. In plastering, coves are

    A. never required
    B. used to obtain an even finish
    C. required where floor and wall meet
    D. sometimes required where wall and ceiling meet

38. Wood bridging should

    A. be nailed top and bottom before placing the subflooring
    B. not be placed until the subflooring is placed
    C. be nailed at its upper end only before the subflooring is placed
    D. be nailed at its lower end only before the subflooring is placed

39. Cross-furring is required by the Code in

    A. walls consisting of 2 x 4 studding
    B. ceilings when lath is attached directly to the wood joists of the floor above
    C. walls using metal lath on wood studs
    D. suspended ceilings

40. Board measure is a measure of

    A. length B. area C. volume D. weight

41. The consistency of concrete is measured by a _____ test.

    A. slump
    B. penetration
    C. strength
    D. time of set

42. Bricking up the space between furring at floors is done to

    A. provide corbelling
    B. fire-stop the wall
    C. stiffen the structure
    D. moisture-proof the wall

43. The dressed size of lumber is

    A. smaller than the nominal size
    B. depends upon the grade of the lumber
    C. its size as finally used on the job
    D. not related to its nominal size

44. Of the following types of joints, the one which is LEAST related to the others is

    A. raked B. weather C. construction D. struck

45. A rowlock course consists of bricks

    A. set on end
    B. set on their sides
    C. set flat
    D. laid alternately as headers and stretchers

46. With respect to flooring, shrinkage in a wood joist is MOST serious in

    A. length
    B. width
    C. depth
    D. all of the above

47. Neat cement and marble chips are used

    A. as mortar in marble walls and floors
    B. to make terrazzo
    C. for stucco
    D. for ornamental ceilings

48. Cinder concrete is sometimes used in floor construction in place of stone concrete because the cinder concrete

    A. permits thinner floors
    B. provides better acoustics
    C. is more fire-resistant
    D. is lighter

49. If a subcontractor's work is unsatisfactory,

    A. inform him that his payments will be withheld
    B. make the subcontractor's foreman rip it out
    C. so inform the general contractor
    D. warn him that further unsatisfactory work will bar him from future city work

50. *Extra work* is work 50.____
    A. not called for in the contract
    B. required to correct unsatisfactory work
    C. done outside of regular hours
    D. required by inexperienced inspectors which is unnecessary

---

KEY (CORRECT ANSWERS)

1. D	11. A	21. D	31. D	41. A
2. B	12. C	22. B	32. C	42. B
3. C	13. A	23. C	33. C	43. A
4. A	14. D	24. C	34. A	44. C
5. C	15. D	25. D	35. B	45. B
6. B	16. C	26. C	36. C	46. C
7. A	17. C	27. D	37. D	47. B
8. D	18. A	28. C	38. C	48. D
9. A	19. A	29. B	39. D	49. C
10. B	20. A	30. C	40. C	50. A

TEST 2

DIRECTIONS: Each question or incomplete statement is followed by several suggested answers or completions. Select the one that BEST answers the question or completes the statement. *PRINT THE LETTER OF THE CORRECT ANSWER IN THE SPACE AT THE RIGHT.*

1. Aggregates used to make concrete do NOT include

    A. sand B. gravel C. cement D. crushed rock

2. Careful slushing of the end joints of slip sills is PRIMARILY required to

    A. prevent displacement
    B. provide water tightness
    C. maintain bond
    D. prevent discoloration

3. The use of bats in brick work is justified when such use

    A. is required by the bond
    B. reduces the amount of face brick
    C. eliminates headers
    D. prevents waste of excess bats

4. In construction work, a neat line is a(n) _____ line.

    A. inside B. outside C. vertical D. center

5. In acceptable concrete practice, a small w/c ratio is MOST likely to indicate that the concrete mix will

    A. be stiff
    B. produce high-strength concrete
    C. have a big slump
    D. produce low-strength concrete

6. In concrete work, wooden form spreaders should be removed

    A. as soon as the concrete is placed
    B. after the concrete has attained initial set
    C. after the concrete has attained final set
    D. after the concrete has attained full strength

7. The rounded, projecting edge of a stair tread is the

    A. coping B. nosing C. rising D. stringing

8. A fire tower differs from fire stairs PRINCIPALLY in

    A. capacity
    B. location
    C. height
    D. tread and riser requirements

9. The area of a circle 2'6" in diameter is, in square feet, MOST NEARLY

    A. 4.6 B. 4.9 C. 5.3 D. 6.7

10. A cantilever beam would MOST likely be used in connection with a

   A. floor opening   B. balcony
   C. warehouse floor   D. roof opening

11. The Code requires various thicknesses of concrete cover for reinforcing rods used in the different elements of a building.
   That element which requires the LEAST cover is

   A. column   B. beam   C. girder   D. flat slab

12. A specification reads: *The span length of freely supported beams shall be the clear span plus the effective depth of beam, but shall be within the distance between centers of supports.*
   According to this specification, the span length of such a beam with an effective depth of 22 inches, supported on 18 inch walls spaced 16'0" in the clear, is

   A. 17'9"   B. 17'7"   C. 17'6"   D. 17'5"

13. Bond plaster would be used

   A. where a fine, hard finish is required
   B. on concrete surfaces
   C. between scratch and finish coats
   D. on certain types of lath

14. A concealed draft opening is MOST closely associated with

   A. ventilation   B. heating
   C. fire-stopping   D. air conditioning

15. In estimating the cost of a reinforced concrete structure, the contractor would be LEAST concerned with

   A. volume of concrete
   B. surface area of forms
   C. pounds of reinforcing steel
   D. type of coarse aggregate

16. A brick wall is to be plastered.
   The BEST type of joint for this surface of the wall is

   A. flush   B. weathered   C. concave   D. raked

17. A groove is cut in the underside of a stone sill to

   A. keep water from the wall
   B. improve the bond with the wall
   C. conceal reinforcing
   D. reduce the weight of the sill

18. Joists spaced 16" o.c. on a 12'0" span support a floor which is to carry a live load of 80 pounds per square foot. The TOTAL live load carried by a single joist is, in pounds,

   A. 590   B. 920   C. 1195   D. 1280

19. Pointing up around the end of a joist resting on a brick wall is

    A. *good,* because it improves appearance
    B. *bad,* because it may cause rotting of joist
    C. *good,* because it results in a more solid wall
    D. *bad,* because it interferes with fire-stopping

20. In a roof, the LONGEST rafters are _____ rafters.

    A. common   B. hip jack
    C. valley jack   D. either hip or valley jack

21. The thickness of lumber used for grounds is USUALLY, in inches,

    A. 7/32   B. 3/4   C. 25/32   D. 15/32

22. The terms *plank, scantling, heavy joists,* when used in connection with lumber, refer to

    A. dimensions   B. use   C. grade   D. finish

23. The Code provides that cold bends in reinforcing bars for concrete work shall have a radius at LEAST equal to the least dimension of the bar multiplied by

    A. 1   B. 2   C. 3   D. 4

24. According to the Code, gas cutting of structural steel is NOT permitted

    A. unless the member cut is carrying stress
    B. in preparation for welding
    C. to replace the milling of surfaces
    D. under any circumstances

25. In building construction, an apron would MOST likely be installed by a

    A. carpenter   B. sheet-metal worker
    C. bricklayer   D. glazier

26. In a building with masonry walls, furring

    A. is of no advantage
    B. is of no help in preventing wetting of plaster
    C. is used only because it provides a nailing surface
    D. adds to the insulating quality of the wall

27. Oil is applied to the inside surfaces of concrete forms PRIMARILY to

    A. make form removal easier
    B. provide a smoother finish to the concrete
    C. prevent leakage of water from the concrete
    D. neutralize acids present in the wood

28. A deformed reinforcing rod is superior to an equivalent smooth rod because it

    A. permits better bond with the concrete
    B. has greater tensile strength
    C. weighs more
    D. is easier to bend

29. In the usual six-story multiple dwelling, fire escapes are 29.____
    A. supported on floor joists cantilevered out through the walls
    B. supported on a framework tied to, but otherwise independent of, the building
    C. hung from the parapet
    D. supported on brackets which are bolted to channels on the innerside of the wall

30. A building on a lot 50'0" wide by 110'0" deep has a rectangular court 37'0" long by 8'6" 30.____
    wide.
    The area of the court is the following percentage of the area of the lot:
    A. 6.4   B. 6.2   C. 5.8   D. 5.7

KEY (CORRECT ANSWERS)

1.	C	16.	D
2.	B	17.	A
3.	A	18.	D
4.	B	19.	B
5.	B	20.	A
6.	A	21.	C
7.	B	22.	A
8.	B	23.	B
9.	B	24.	C
10.	B	25.	A
11.	D	26.	D
12.	C	27.	A
13.	B	28.	A
14.	C	29.	D
15.	D	30.	D

EXAMINATION SECTION
TEST 1

DIRECTIONS: Each question or incomplete statement is followed by several suggested answers or completions. Select the one that BEST answers the question or completes the statement. *PRINT THE LETTER OF THE CORRECT ANSWER IN THE SPACE AT THE RIGHT.*

1. Of the following reasons for inspection of construction, the one that applies MOST to inspectors in the department is to

    A. coordinate work of the different crafts
    B. avoid extra construction costs
    C. insure adherence to standards of materials and craftsmanship
    D. speed completion of the work

    1.____

2. Of the following statements, the one that is CORRECT is that it is

    A. not important for an inspector to maintain good, personal relations with contractors because contractors might attempt to take advantage of the inspector
    B. important for an inspector to maintain good personal relations with contractors because it will then be easier to obtain cooperation from them
    C. not important for an inspector to maintain good personal relations with contractors because contractors must comply with the Code in any case
    D. important for an inspector to maintain good personal relations with contractors because the inspector can then eliminate much of the required inspections

    2.____

3. Contractors will many times insist on discussing problems only with the senior construction inspector rather than the district inspector.
   This practice is

    A. *good,* because the contractor will get the correct answer immediately
    B. *poor,* because it tends to undermine the responsibility of the district inspector
    C. *good,* because this gives the senior construction inspector an opportunity to train the men under him
    D. *poor,* because the senior construction inspector cannot be familiar with all the conditions in his area.

    3.____

4. It has been said that the perfect job has never been built. Where litigation with respect to a job arises, the BEST indications that the inspector has made proper inspections are the

    A. statements made by the builder
    B. inspector's district assignments
    C. number of violations filed in a district
    D. inspector's written reports

    4.____

5. Defective material should be removed from the job site immediately.
   The MAIN reason for this is to

    A. prevent accidents due to poor *housekeeping*
    B. prevent *accidental* use of the defective material in the construction

    5.____

89

C. protect the department from any claim against the department
D. insure that the builder does not make the same mistake again

6. A senior inspector should always explain to newly appointed inspectors the importance of the work to be done by them. The MAIN reason for this is that

   A. the inspectors know what has to be done
   B. if this is not done, inspectors will skip unimportant inspections
   C. an inspector who understands the value of proper inspections will most likely do a better job
   D. inspectors will then not have an excuse for making improper inspections

7. Assume that you find that the inspections and reports made by a newly appointed inspector are consistently below a reasonable standard.
   You should FIRST

   A. ask that the inspector be reassigned to a task he can perform properly
   B. request that the inspector be brought up on charges
   C. prepare a formal memorandum stating the facts so that your superiors will be aware of the situation
   D. try to determine and correct the cause for the sub-standard performance

8. In introducing new policies to inspectors under them, senior inspectors should

   A. describe the new policy in detail to each man individually so that the senior is sure the man knows it
   B. describe the new policy to the men and explain the necessity of the new policy
   C. tell the men your honest opinion of the policy, but also tell them it is the department's orders and must be followed
   D. give the men the new policy in writing so that there can be no excuse that they misunderstood you

9. Cooperation from inspectors working under you can BEST be secured by

   A. siding with the inspectors whenever they have a complaint
   B. being a stern disciplinarian and not letting the inspectors get away with anything
   C. emphasizing to the inspectors that if they want anything done for them, they must come to you
   D. being willing to listen to the inspectors, and helping them where possible

10. It is considered good practice for a supervisor to encourage his subordinates to discuss and participate in the solution of problems.
    The MAIN reason for this is that

    A. the subordinate generally knows more about the individual problem than the supervisor
    B. then two people can share the responsibility instead of only one
    C. this will Increase the job satisfaction of the men and improve morale
    D. it will reduce the work load of the supervisor so that he can spend more time on more important matters

11. Of the following, the one MOST important quality required of a good supervisor is 11.____

    A. ambition   B. leadership   C. friendliness   D. popularity

12. When an inspector submits a poorly written report, the senior inspector should 12.____

    A. discuss the report with the inspector as soon as possible after it has been submitted
    B. call a meeting of all inspectors to explain how reports should be written
    C. wait a few days to see if other reports turned in by the inspector are written the same way
    D. rewrite the report properly himself

13. A senior inspector who is very lenient with his men will find A senior inspector who is very lenient with his men will find that 13.____

    A. the men will cooperate more readily with him
    B. there will be a higher quality of performance from the men
    C. the men will have less respect for the senior inspector
    D. the men will get along better among themselves

14. It is often said that a supervisor can delegate authority, but never responsibility. This means MOST NEARLY that 14.____

    A. a supervisor must do his own work if he expects it to be done properly
    B. a supervisor can assign some one else to do his work, but in the last analysis, the supervisor himself must take the blame for any actions followed
    C. authority and responsibility are two separate things that cannot be borne by the same person
    D. it is better for a supervisor never to delegate his authority

15. Of the following, the MOST important characteristic of a good senior inspector is 15.____

    A. the ability to make friends with the men under him
    B. fairness in dealing with the men under him
    C. willingness to be on the men's side in their complaints against the Department
    D. willingness to overlook mistakes made by the men under him

16. The BEST relationship between the senior inspector and his inspectors exist when 16.____

    A. they stick together against adverse criticism made by the department heads
    B. the senior inspector respects the inspectors' rights
    C. the senior inspector will *cover* for the inspectors' faults
    D. the senior inspector avoids enforcing the rules he knows the men do not like

17. With regard to public relations, the MOST important item should be emphasized in an employee training program is that 17.____

    A. each inspector is a public relations agent
    B. an inspector should give the public all the information it asks for
    C. it is better to make mistakes and give erroneous information then to tell the public that you do not know the correct answer to their problem
    D. public relations is so specialized a field that only persons specially trained in it should consider it

18. Senior inspectors should regularly visit the districts covered by the inspectors under them in order to

    A. make sure their inspectors know that they are being watched
    B. give people an opportunity to speak directly to the *person in charge*
    C. observe the work of their inspectors to see that they meet proper standards
    D. get the public acquainted with them

19. The one of the following statements that is CORRECT is:

    A. When a stupid question is asked of you by the public, it should be disregarded.
    B. If you insist on formality between you and the public, the public will not be able to ask stupid questions that cannot be answered.
    C. The public should be treated courteously, regardless of how stupid their questions may be.
    D. You should explain to the public how stupid their questions are.

20. Assume that during field inspections, senior inspectors are constantly being asked questions about their job.
    In this respect, the inspector should remember that

    A. entering into conversation with people not connected with the job will leave the impression that city employees do little work
    B. efficiency can best be demonstrated by appearing to be too busy to answer questions
    C. supervisors should take every opportunity to tell the public how busy they really are
    D. the attitudes of the public are often formed by their personal contact's with city employees

21. The condition MOST likely to improve the morale of the inspectional force is

    A. liberal time allowances
    B. recognition of each individual's own efforts by the department
    C. overlooking of minor infractions of rules
    D. allowing the men to do the job in whatever manner they feel proper

22. As a senior inspector, you find that, in error you have reprimanded one of your inspectors.
    You should

    A. ignore the error, but be more careful in the future
    B. make up for it in the future by ignoring his next mistake
    C. find something else wrong
    D. apologize to the man for your mistake

23. As a senior inspector, assume that you have to settle a complaint made by a property owner against one of your inspectors. The PROPER thing to do would be to

    A. back up your inspector, telling the owner he is wrong
    B. tell the owner you will protect him against unjustified violations
    C. listen to both inspector and owner to get at the truth
    D. tell the owner you will check into the matter at your earliest convenience

24. Assume a suggestion is made by one of your inspectors for improving inspectional procedures.
    Of the following, the BEST course to follow is to

    A. tell the inspector that the present method used has always been followed and is therefore the best way
    B. check the inspector's suggestion, and if it is good pass it on to the chief inspector
    C. have the man write a report to the superintendent with regard to the suggestion
    D. hold a meeting with the other inspectors to see whether they like the suggestion

25. With respect to anonymous complaints, it is

    A. *good practice* to investigate them since they may be valid
    B. *poor practice* to investigate them since anyone who is not honest enough to sign his name is probably just a trouble maker
    C. *good practice* to investigate them to keep your inspectors *on their toes*
    D. *poor practice* to investigate them since this gives your inspectors the feeling they are being spied upon

26. Members of the public frequently ask about departmental procedures.
    Of the following, it is BEST to

    A. advise the public to put the question in writing so that he can get a proper formal reply
    B. refuse to answer, because this is a confidential matter
    C. explain the procedure as briefly as possible
    D. attempt to avoid the issue by discussing other matters

27. In making an inspection on an alteration job, you should

    A. avoid conversation with the foreman on the job
    B. try to get the foreman to talk as much as possible so that he will tell you all the things that are wrong with the job
    C. give the appearance of listening to the foreman but actually ignoring most of what he says
    D. listen to what the foreman has to say, but discourage undue conversation

28. Of the following, the one that would LEAST likely occur as a result of planning of your work is

    A. anticipation of problems before they occur
    B. necessity of frequently putting in overtime to solve problems
    C. better job coordination
    D. ability to meet deadlines for reports

29. In evaluating the quality of an inspector, a senior inspector should be LEAST interested in

    A. whether the man is adaptable to different situations
    B. the man's dependability
    C. how the man gets along with his co-workers and the public
    D. the number of reports the man turns in

30. In instituting disciplinary action against an inspector, the senior inspector should avoid 30.____
    A. taking extenuating circumstances into account
    B. explaining the serious consequences of the infraction
    C. being firm and positive
    D. delay once a decision is reached

KEY (CORRECT ANSWERS)

1.	C	16.	B
2.	B	17.	A
3.	B	18.	C
4.	D	19.	C
5.	B	20.	D
6.	C	21.	B
7.	D	22.	D
8.	B	23.	C
9.	D	24.	B
10.	C	25.	A
11.	B	26.	C
12.	A	27.	D
13.	C	28.	B
14.	B	29.	D
15.	B	30.	D

EXAMINATION SECTION
TEST 1

DIRECTIONS: Each question or incomplete statement is followed by several suggested answers or completions. Select the one that BEST answers the question or completes the statement. *PRINT THE LETTER OF THE CORRECT ANSWER IN THE SPACE AT THE RIGHT.*

1. A percentage of the payment for a contract is held back until the job is completed for one year.
   The MAIN reason for this practice is to insure that the

   A. city doesn't overpay the contractor for the job
   B. contractor will return to correct defective work after the job is completed
   C. contractor will not make unwarranted claims against the city
   D. contractor will pay all his subcontractors

2. There are four separate major contracts on a certain building construction project.
   The MAJOR disadvantage of this practice, as compared to the practice of having a single contract, is

   A. the difficulty in coordinating the work
   B. the low level of productivity of the tradesman
   C. cost of the material going into the building is greater
   D. the difficulty in finding competent bidders on the contracts

3. Of the following, the PREFERRED way to authorize a contractor to perform work other than required by the contract is by a

   A. T & M order   B. unit price order
   C. lump sum modification D. change order

4. A contract requires that the prime contractor do a certain minimum percentage of the work with his own forces.
   Of the following, the BEST reason for this requirement is to

   A. insure good work
   B. discourage bidders who may not have the ability to do the job
   C. encourage more people to bid the job, thus lowering the bid price
   D. freeze out incompetent subcontractors

5. In computing an extra based on the actual cost of work done, the THREE MAJOR items that go into the cost are

   A. taxes, labor, and material
   B. time, taxes, and material
   C. labor, material, and equipment
   D. taxes, labor, and equipment

6. A contractor is to be penalized if he exceeds a certain completion date. There is a major strike lasting a month that shuts down all construction.
   Under these conditions, the completion date should be

A. held unchanged
B. made two weeks later than the original date
C. made one month later than the original date
D. made six weeks later than the original completion date

7. The one of the following that refers to a Federal safety program in construction is

    A. OSHA   B. AISC   C. AIEE   D. UL

8. With regard to the placing of concrete, the contractor is GENERALLY

    A. limited to a specific method by the contract
    B. not permitted to rent equipment to place the concrete
    C. not permitted to pump the concrete into place
    D. permitted to choose his own method of placing the concrete

9. The MOST practical control the inspector or resident engineer has over the contractor when the inspector is not satisfied with the quality of the work is to

    A. discuss withholding payment on that part of the work that is unsatisfactory
    B. threaten to have the contractor thrown off the job
    C. request that the contractor fire the men responsible for the unsatisfactory work
    D. call the owner of the company and explain the situation to him

10. The MOST practical method of being sure that the architect will be satisfied with the appearance of the exterior brick work for a building is to

    A. build a sample wall section, for the architect's approval, with the brick that is delivered to the job site
    B. send the architect to the plant supplying the brick to insure that the color and tone of the brick is satisfactory
    C. have the architect's representative on the job while the brick work is being erected to be sure the finished product is satisfactory
    D. put a damage clause in the contract penalizing the contractor if the brick work is not satisfactory to the architect

11. Of the following, the MOST frequent problem that will arise during the construction of a building is

    A. inability to fit all the reinforcing steel in the space allotted to it
    B. interference in piping and ductwork
    C. inability to keep walls level
    D. settling of the foundation as the load comes on the building

12. To find the number of reinforcing bars that should be in a slab, the inspector SHOULD refer to the

    A. architect's plan
    B. reinforcing steel design drawings
    C. standard detail drawings
    D. reinforcing steel detail drawings

13. The specifications for a building state that a certain brick type shall be *Stark Brick type XX or equal.*
    The BEST reason for inserting the *or equal* clause is to

    A. permit other companies to compete in supplying the brick
    B. allow other companies to submit their product to determine which is best
    C. limit the suppliers only to those companies whose product is superior to that produced by Stark
    D. allow Stark Brick Company to set the standard for the industry

14. In the absence of a formal training program for inspectors, the BEST of the following ways to train a new man who is to do inspection work is to

    A. give him the literature on the subject so that he can learn what he has to know
    B. have him accompany an inspector as the inspector does his work so that he can learn by observing
    C. assign him the job and let him learn on his own
    D. tell him to go to a school at night that specializes in this field so that he will gain the necessary background

15. Of the following, the safety practice that is REQUIRED on the construction job site is

    A. safety shoes must be worn by all workers
    B. safety goggles must be worn by all workers
    C. safety helmets must be worn by all workers
    D. all workers must have a safety kit in their possession

16. Safety on the job is the concern of

    A. the individual workman only
    B. the contractor only
    C. all parties on the job
    D. the insuring company only

17. Frequently, payments due the contractor are delayed many months because of a backlog of work in the agency.
    This practice is considered

    A. *good* because the city saves money by delaying payment
    B. *poor* because the contractors will raise their bids in the future to compensate for the added cost
    C. *poor* because it becomes difficult to compute payments
    D. *good* because it forces the contractor to do good work in order to be sure that he will receive payment

18. Provisions are made in a contract for payment for certain items when delivered to the job before installation.
    The MAIN reason for this practice is to

    A. enable better inspection of the items
    B. prevent bottlenecks during construction
    C. give the contractor a quick profit on the items
    D. allow the contractor more time to shop for the items

4 (#1)

19. The agency that approves payments to building contractors is the 19.____

    A. Corporation Counsel   B. Comptroller's Office
    C. Board of Estimate   D. City Planning Commission

20. The bond that the contractor puts up to insure that he will start work is the 20.____

    A. Bid Bond   B. Payment Bond
    C. Performance Bond   D. Liability Insurance

21. Of the following, the BEST practice to follow in order to minimize claims of damage to adjacent buildings during the construction of a building is to 21.____

    A. take out special insurance against such claims
    B. make a detailed survey of the condition of the nearby buildings before construction begins
    C. make a payment to adjacent property owners in advance so that they waive claims of damage to their property
    D. have the buildings underpinned

22. The four MAJOR contracts on a building project are: 22.____

    A. General Construction, Electrical, Plumbing and Drainage, Heating, Ventilating and Air Conditioning
    B. Plumbing, Heating and Ventilating, Air Conditioning, and General Construction
    C. Foundations, Superstructure, Mechanical, and Electrical
    D. Air Conditioning, Electrical, Mechanical, and Structural

23. Oil tanks, when set in place inside a building, are frequently filled with water. 23.____
    The BEST reason for this practice is

    A. to prevent them from floating off their foundation if water fills the room
    B. to enable them to be lifted up more easily
    C. to prevent them from becoming rusted
    D. for emergency use in case of fire

24. The filing system used in the field for correspondence is required to be uniform for all jobs. 24.____
    The BEST reason for this requirement is that

    A. there is only one good way of setting up the filing system
    B. the standardized system is compact, thereby saving space
    C. other interested parties such as engineers from the main office will be able to use the files
    D. the contractor's forces will understand the filing system and will be able to extract necessary correspondence

25. Upon excavation to the subgrade of a footing to be placed on piles, the inspector finds that the soil is very poor. 25.____
    Of the following, the PROPER action for the inspector to take is to

    A. do nothing
    B. add 20% to the number of piles
    C. notify the engineer's office of this condition
    D. order the contractor to keep excavating until he hits better soil

26. The general contractor is required to submit a progress schedule before starting work. Of the following, the BEST reason for this requirement is to

    A. determine if the contractor intends to complete the job
    B. enable the inspector to determine whether the contractor is on schedule
    C. enable the inspector to estimate monthly payments
    D. check minority hiring

27. If a contractor is falling behind schedule, the FIRST thing to check if the inspector is looking for the cause of this condition is the

    A. number of men he has on the job
    B. efficiency of his crew
    C. availability of equipment needed to do the job
    D. availability of the latest drawings needed by the contractor

28. The critical path method is a method for

    A. finding the best material needed for a specific use
    B. determining the best arrangement of equipment
    C. determining the best time to replace a piece of machinery
    D. scheduling work

29. The contractor states to the inspector that a given structural detail is undersized and unsafe.
    Of the following, the BEST action for the inspector to take in this situation is to

    A. ignore the complaint since the contractor is not an engineer
    B. change the detail by issuing a change order
    C. notify your superiors of the contractor's statements
    D. allow the contractor to modify the detail since it is his responsibility

30. The contractor proposes to use an additive to the concrete to accelerate its set. He asks you, the inspector, for permission to use it.
    Of the following, the FIRST action to take in response to his request is to

    A. check if the use of the additive is permitted by the specifications
    B. tell him to put the request in writing
    C. ask your superior if the use of the additive is acceptable
    D. deny him permission since additives to concrete are not permitted

KEY (CORRECT ANSWERS)

1.	B	16.	C
2.	A	17.	B
3.	D	18.	B
4.	B	19.	B
5.	C	20.	A
6.	C	21.	B
7.	A	22.	A
8.	D	23.	A
9.	A	24.	C
10.	A	25.	A
11.	B	26.	B
12.	D	27.	A
13.	A	28.	D
14.	B	29.	C
15.	C	30.	A

EXAMINATION SECTION
TEST 1

DIRECTIONS: Each question or incomplete statement is followed by several suggested answers or completions. Select the one that BEST answers the question or completes the statement. *PRINT THE LETTER OF THE CORRECT ANSWER IN THE SPACE AT THE RIGHT.*

1. It is generally recommended that bid security in a construction contract should NOT be less than _____ percent of the amount of the bid. 1._____

   A. 5 B. 10 C. 15 D. 20

2. Which of the following is NOT a Division 4 item according to the CSI Masterformat for specifications? 2._____

   A. Concrete
   B. Stone
   C. Masonry restoration and cleaning
   D. Refractories

3. What is the term for the written documents which describe the rights, responsibilities, and relationships of the contracting parties? 3._____

   A. Contract documents   B. General conditions
   C. Standard documents   D. Specifications

4. Which of the following is most likely to be covered under a contractor's comprehensive general liability insurance policy? 4._____

   A. Injury to the contractor's own employees
   B. Damage to underground utilities
   C. Damage to property under the care, custody or control of the contractor
   D. Bodily injury to visitors of the construction site

5. Generally, which of the following types of contracts presents the fewest difficulties in dealing with change orders? 5._____

   A. Unit-price   B. Cost-plus-fee
   C. Lump-sum   D. Cost-plus-award

6. Which of the following performance characteristics is associated with fire safety in construction specifications? 6._____

   A. Air infiltration   B. Thermal expansion
   C. Toxicity   D. Water vapor transmission

7. The acceptance period most commonly used in the bidding process of construction projects is a period of _____ days. 7._____

   A. 10 B. 30 C. 60 D. 90

8. Each of the following is an advantage associated with the use of product approval standards in construction contract specifications EXCEPT 8._____

A. the architect has control over the products used
B. it discourages bid peddling or shopping
C. complete flexibility in contracting the arrangement
D. it limits the number of products that can be specified

9. If a retainage arrangement has been made part of a construction contract, what percent is usually held by the owner until final payment is made? 9._____

   A. 5   B. 10   C. 25   D. 50

10. Of the following construction specifications, which is most effectively written? 10._____

    A. Install glass panels on both sides of main entrance
    B. Glass panels shall be installed on both sides of main entrance
    C. Glass panels shall be installed on either side of main entrance
    D. Glass panels shall be installed by a licensed workman on both sides of main entrance

11. In general, the use of a subcontractor listing requirement in the bidding process is favored by each of the following: 11._____
    I. Owners
    II. Prime contractors
    III. Subcontractors
    The CORRECT answer is:

    A. I only   B. II only   C. III only   D. I, III

12. A base bid specification used in a construction contract 12._____

    A. specifies only one brand name or proprietary make for each individual material, piece of equipment or product
    B. is written without reference to brand names or proprietary makes
    C. names two or more brand names or proprietary makes for each item the architect or engineer wishes to use
    D. includes a list of substitutions

13. Which of the following statements is true concerning the use of the double form of bonds as surety regarding a construction contract? 13._____

    A. It presents a potential conflict of interest between the owner and persons furnishing labor and materials.
    B. The premium cost of the bond protection is higher than the single form.
    C. It covers separately the interests of the owner and of subcontractors, material suppliers, and workmen.
    D. The face value of the bond can be consumed entirely by the owner, since the owner's interest takes priority.

14. Each of the following is an element that is typically included in an Invitation to Bid EXCEPT 14._____

    A. acknowledgement
    B. guarantee bonds
    C. time and place for receipt of bids
    D. examination and procurement of documents

15. Under most construction contracts, an owner will have a right of action against a contrac- 15.____
tor beyond the warranty period if the

    A. contractor's inadequate performance is a result of insufficient plans and specifications that were not prepared by the contractor or with the contractor's guarantee of adequacy
    B. contractor's inadequate performance is latent in nature and could not have been detected by the owner during ordinary use and maintenance of the structure
    C. nature of the contractor's inadequate performance is not specifically named in the terms of the performance bond
    D. contractor has been grossly negligent

16. In performance specifying, what is the term for a qualitative statement of the desired per- 16.____
formance?

    A. Requirement   B. Criterion
    C. Test   D. Standard

17. Which of the following is a nontechnical paragraph that would appear in a technical sec- 17.____
tion that is included in a book of specifications?

    A. Workmanship
    B. Samples and shop drawings
    C. Schedules
    D. General requirements

18. In cases where the courts are consulted to grant a contractor relief from a bid that was 18.____
submitted in error, the most likely result is that the contractor

    A. must forfeit the entire amount of bid security to the owner
    B. is permitted to submit a corrected bid without penalty
    C. is permitted only to withdraw the bid without penalty
    D. is permitted to submit a corrected bid after forfeiting a nominal amount of bid security

19. Which of the following is least likely to result in a claim dispute between the contractor 19.____
and an owner?

    A. Rejection of subcontractor
    B. Changed conditions
    C. Acceleration
    D. Rejection of *or-equal* substitutions

20. Which of the following is MOST likely to be considered an excusable cause of delay by 20.____
the contractor under the terms of a construction contract?

    A. Adverse weather
    B. Labor strike
    C. Insufficient estimate of required materials
    D. Insufficient labor pool

21. In the bidding documents of a construction contract, which of the following elements would typically appear in the Instructions to Bidders?

    A. Agreement to accept contract
    B. Bid schedule
    C. Project identification
    D. Reform of bid

22. Target estimates are not typically involved in the negotiation or bidding of _____ contracts.

    A. cost-plus-fixed-fee   B. lump-sum
    C. cost-plus-percentage   D. unit-price

23. A _____ bond is given by a developer to a public body to guarantee construction of all necessary improvements and utilities.

    A. subdivision   B. license
    C. fidelity   D. discharge

24. Of the following, which Division heading would appear latest in the CSI Masterformat of construction specifications?

    A. Furnishings   B. Special Construction
    C. Electrical   D. Equipment

25. Each of the following is typically included in a contract's bidding requirements EXCEPT

    A. bid forms
    B. specifications
    C. instructions to bidders
    D. information available to bidders

KEY (CORRECT ANSWERS)

1.	A	11.	D
2.	A	12.	A
3.	B	13.	C
4.	D	14.	A
5.	B	15.	B
6.	C	16.	A
7.	B	17.	B
8.	D	18.	C
9.	B	19.	A
10.	A	20.	B

21. D
22. B
23. A
24. C
25. B

TEST 2

DIRECTIONS: Each question or incomplete statement is followed by several suggested answers or completions. Select the one that BEST answers the question or completes the statement. *PRINT THE LETTER OF THE CORRECT ANSWER IN THE SPACE AT THE RIGHT.*

1. Each of the following is a common motivation for a contractor's submission of an unbalanced bid on a project EXCEPT to

    A. distribute fixed costs properly over the true quantities of work when errors are perceived in the quantities listed on the proposal form
    B. increase the percentage in a cost-plus-percentage project
    C. increase profit, especially on quantities that have been underestimated by the owner
    D. make early progress payments large enough to minimize the contractor's initial costs

    1.____

2. When specifications in construction contracts are written without reference to brand names or proprietary makes, they are known as _____ specifications.

    A. open
    B. base bid
    C. bidder's choice
    D. alternate listing

    2.____

3. Of the following types of hold-harmless clauses, _____ indemnification used in construction contracts holds the owner and architect-engineer harmless against any claims caused by the negligence of the prime contractor or subcontractor.

    A. exclusive
    B. limited-form
    C. intermediate-form
    D. broad-form

    3.____

4. In the CSI Masterformat of specifications, plumbing is a construction item that is described under the heading of

    A. metals
    B. mechanical
    C. specialties
    D. special construction

    4.____

5. Which of the following are generally true of unit-price contracts?
    I. Units of work are estimated before project operations begin and are not allowed to vary thereafter.
    II. The unit costs of items in the contract documents are indeterminable until the project is completed.
    III. The total sum of money paid to the contractor for each work item remains indeterminable until completion of the project.

    The CORRECT answer is:

    A. I only   B. III only   C. I, II   D. II, III

    5.____

6. Which of the following phrases appearing in construction specifications is most potentially troublesome?

    A. Contractor shall
    B. Free of defect
    C. Guaranteed
    D. Or equal

    6.____

106

7. For a contractor to bind a subcontractor to its initial subbid on the basis that the contractor relied on this bid in submitting its own project proposal, the contractor should have

   A. asked the subcontractor to verify the subbid's correctness in advance
   B. located evidence that the subcontractor has submitted unresponsive bids in the past
   C. delayed accepting the subcontractor's bid after its own bid is accepted by the owner
   D. announced a *freeze* on subcontractor bids before submitting its own bid proposal

8. Typically, the preliminary project description, a written document that records early decisions about major project elements, is recorded during the _____ phase of document preparation.

   A. schematic design
   B. bidding
   C. design-development
   D. construction documents

9. In the bidding documents of a typical construction contract, which of the following elements is included in the Bid Form?

   A. Conditions under which bids can be rejected
   B. Guarantee bonds
   C. Alternates
   D. The procedure under which the award to contract will be made

10. Under the terms of a typical construction project, the contractor may be held to guarantee that the completed project
    I. is free of defects in design
    II. has been executed with the quality of workmanship and materials specified in the contract documents
    III. will accomplish the intended purpose
    The CORRECT answer is:

    A. I only B. II only C. III only D. II, III

11. Which of the following descriptions would appear LAST in a technical section that is written according to the CSI standard format?

    A. Examination
    B. Summary
    C. Schedules
    D. Definitions

12. _____ clauses are used in construction contracts to eliminate or modify contract provisions that add cost to a project but are not necessary to the structure's required performance, safety, appearance, or maintenance.

    A. Escape
    B. Changed-conditions
    C. Value engineering
    D. Escalation

13. Standard documents which are incorporated by citation in the bidding and contract documents are known as

    A. general conditions
    B. specifications
    C. reference documents
    D. drawings

14. If addenda to a construction contract are included in a project manual, they usually appear

    A. at the very beginning, after the title page
    B. between the table of contents and the bidding requirements
    C. between the conditions of the contract and the schedule of drawings
    D. at the very end

15. Which of the following would most likely be included in a *changed-conditions* clause in a construction contract?

    A. Subsurface soil conditions
    B. Conditions resulting from drought
    C. Conditions resulting from flood
    D. Nonphysical conditions

16. What type of specification refers to a standard established for either a material, a test method or an insulation procedure?

    A. Proprietary   B. Descriptive
    C. Performance   D. Reference

17. In a contract bond arrangement, the _____ is the obligee.

    A. owner   B. surety company
    C. architect-engineer   D. contractor

18. Specifications that are written into a construction contract should usually be formatted in the _____ style.

    A. indented   B. modified block
    C. block   D. centered

19. When several alternates are listed on the base bid for a lump-sum project submitted by a contractor, it may be possible for an owner to juggle acceptance of the alternates so that a preferred contractor receives the contract. The best way to safeguard against this possibility is for the bidding documents to

    A. prohibit the use of alternatives altogether
    B. state the order of acceptance of the alternatives
    C. limit the use of alternates to scope of construction, rather than methods or materials
    D. limit the use of alternates to materials

20. Which of the following is NOT an *XCU* exclusion from property damage liability coverage under the terms of most construction contracts?

    A. Damage caused by flooding
    B. Underground damage caused by and occurring during the use of mechanical equipment
    C. Collapse or structural damage to any building or structure
    D. Explosion or blasting

21. In the CSI Masterformat of specifications, the item *window treatments* would be described under which of the following headings?

    A. Specialties
    B. Thermal and moisture protection
    C. Furnishings
    D. Doors and windows

    21.____

22. In writing construction specifications, each of the following performance characteristics is associated with compatibility EXCEPT

    A. chemical interaction
    B. dimensional stability
    C. differential thermal movement
    D. galvanic interaction

    22.____

23. When the drawings and specifications are not complete at the time of negotiation of a cost-plus contract, the owner and contractor negotiate what is commonly called a(n)

    A. encumbrance
    B. adhesion contract
    C. scope contract
    D. arbitration

    23.____

24. In a typical *Invitation to Bid*, which of the following elements would typically appear first?

    A. Bid security
    B. Type of contract
    C. Project description
    D. Identification of Principals

    24.____

25. Each of the following is a responsibility bestowed upon the owner in typical construction contracts EXCEPT

    A. securing and paying for necessary easements
    B. assuming liability for negligent acts committed by the contractor in the course of operations
    C. furnishing property surveys that describe and locate project site
    D. providing certain types of insurance

    25.____

KEY (CORRECT ANSWERS)

1. B	11. C	21. C
2. A	12. C	22. B
3. B	13. C	23. C
4. B	14. B	24. D
5. B	15. A	25. B
6. D	16. D	
7. A	17. A	
8. A	18. C	
9. C	19. B	
10. B	20. A	

EXAMINATION SECTION
TEST 1

DIRECTIONS: Each question or incomplete statement is followed by several suggested answers or completions. Select the one that BEST answers the question or completes the statement. *PRINT THE LETTER OF THE CORRECT ANSWER IN THE SPACE AT THE RIGHT.*

1. Of the following, the one MOST important quality required of a good supervisor is
   A. ambition   B. leadership   C. friendliness   D. popularity

2. It is often said that a supervisor can delegate authority but never responsibility. This means MOST NEARLY that
   A. a supervisor must do his own work if he expects it to be done properly
   B. a supervisor can assign someone else to do his work, but in the last analysis, the supervisor himself must take the blame for any actions followed
   C. authority and responsibility are two separate things that cannot be borne by the same person
   D. it is better for a supervisor never to delegate his authority

3. One of your men who is a habitual complainer asks you to grant him a minor privilege.
   Before granting or denying such a request, you should consider
   A. the merits of the case
   B. that it is good for group morale to grant a request of this nature
   C. the man's seniority
   D. that to deny such a request will lower your standing with the men

4. A supervisory practice on the part of a foreman which is MOST likely to lead to confusion and inefficiency is for him to
   A. give orders verbally directly to the man assigned to the job
   B. issue orders only in writing
   C. follow up his orders after issuing them
   D. relay his orders to the men through co-workers

5. It would be POOR supervision on a foreman's part if he
   A. asked an experienced maintainer for his opinion on the method of doing a special job
   B. make it a policy to avoid criticizing a man in front of his co-workers
   C. consulted his assistant supervisor on unusual problems
   D. allowed a cooling-off period of several days before giving one of his men a deserved reprimand

6. Of the following behavior characteristics of a supervisor, the one that is MOST likely to lower the morale of the men he supervises is
   A. diligence
   B. favoritism
   C. punctuality
   D. thoroughness

7. Of the following, the BEST method of getting an employee who is not working up to his capacity to produce more work is to
   A. have another employee criticize his production
   B. privately criticize his production but encourage him to produce more
   C. criticize his production before his associates
   D. criticize his production and threaten to fire him

8. Of the following, the BEST thing for a supervisor to do when a subordinate has done a very good job is to
   A. tell him to take it easy
   B. praise his work
   C. reduce his workload
   D. say nothing because he may become conceited

9. Your orders to your crew are MOST likely to be followed if you
   A. explain the reasons for these orders
   B. warn that all violators will be punished
   C. promise easy assignments to those who follow these orders best
   D. say that they are for the good of the department

10. In order to be a good supervisor, you should
    A. impress upon your men that you demand perfection in their work at all times
    B. avoid being blamed for your crew's mistakes
    C. impress your superior with your ability
    D. see to it that your men get what they are entitled to

11. In giving instructions to a crew, you should
    A. speak in as loud a tone as possible
    B. speak in a coaxing, persuasive manner
    C. speak quietly, clearly, and courteously
    D. always use the word *please* when giving instructions

12. Of the following factors, the one which is LEAST important in evaluating an employee and his work is his
    A. dependability
    B. quantity of work done
    C. quality of work done
    D. education and training

13. When a District Superintendent first assumes his command, it is LEAST important for him at the beginning to observe
    A. how his equipment is designed and its adaptability
    B. how to reorganize the district for greater efficiency
    C. the capabilities of the men in the district
    D. the methods of operation being employed

14. When making an inspection of one of the buildings under your supervision, the BEST procedure to follow in making a record of the inspection is to
    A. return immediately to the office and write a report from memory
    B. write down all the important facts during or as soon as you complete the inspection
    C. fix in your mind all important facts so that you can repeat them from memory if necessary
    D. fix in your mind all important facts so that you can make out your report at the end of the day

14.____

15. Assume that your superior has directed you to make certain changes in your established procedure. After using this modified procedure on several occasions, you find that the original procedure was distinctly superior and you wish to return to it.
    You should
    A. let your superior find this out for himself
    B. simply change back to the original procedure
    C. compile definite data and information to prove your case to your superior
    D. persuade one of the more experienced workers to take this matter up with your superior

15.____

16. An inspector visited a large building under construction. He inspected the soil lines at 9 A.M., water lines at 10 A.M., fixtures at 11 A.M., and did his office work in the afternoon. He followed the same pattern daily for weeks.
    This procedure was
    A. *good*, because it was methodical and he did not miss anything
    B. *good*, because it gave equal time to all phases of the plumbing
    C. *bad*, because not enough time was devoted to fixtures
    D. *bad*, because the tradesmen knew when the inspection would occur

16.____

17. Assume that one of the foremen in a training course, which you are conducting, proposes a poor solution for a maintenance problem.
    Of the following, the BEST course of action for you to take is to
    A. accept the solution tentatively and correct it during the next class meeting
    B. point out all the defects of this proposed solution and wait until somebody thinks of a better solution
    C. try to get the class to reject this proposed solution and develop a better solution
    D. let the matter pass since somebody will present a better solution as the class work proceeds

17.____

18. As a supervisor, you should be seeking ways to improve the efficiency of shop operations by means such as changing established work procedures.
    The following are offered as possible actions that you should consider in changing established work procedures:
    I. Make changes only when your foremen agree to them
    II. Discuss changes with your supervisor before putting them into practice

18.____

III. Standardize any operation which is performed on a continuing basis
IV. Make changes quickly and quietly in order to avoid dissent
V. Secure expert guidance before instituting unfamiliar procedures
Of the following suggested answers, the one that describes the actions to be taken to change established work procedures is
 A. I, IV, V B. II, III, V C. III, IV, V D. All of the above

19. A supervisor determined that a foreman, without informing his superior, delegated responsibility for checking time cards to a member of his gang. The supervisor then called the foreman into his office where he reprimanded the foreman.
This action of the supervisor in reprimanding the foreman was
 A. *proper*, because the checking of time cards is the foreman's responsibility and should not be delegated
 B. *proper*, because the foreman did not ask the supervisor for permission to delegate responsibility
 C. *improper*, because the foreman may no longer take the initiative in solving future problems
 D. *improper*, because the supervisor is interfering in a function which is not his responsibility

20. A capable supervisor should check all operations under his control.
Of the following, the LEAST important reason for doing this is to make sure that
 A. operations are being performed as scheduled
 B. he personally observes all operations at all times
 C. all the operations are still needed
 D. his manpower is being utilized efficiently

21. A supervisor makes it a practice to apply fair and firm discipline in all cases of rule infractions, including those of a minor nature.
This practice should PRIMARILY be considered
 A. *bad*, since applying discipline for minor violations is a waste of time
 B. *good*, because not applying discipline for minor infractions can lead to a more serious erosion of discipline
 C. *bad*, because employees do not like to be disciplined for minor violations of the rules
 D. *good*, because violating any rule can cause a dangerous situation to occur

22. A maintainer would PROPERLY consider it poor supervisory practice for a foreman to consult with him on
 A. which of several repair jobs should be scheduled first
 B. how to cope with personal problems at home
 C. whether the neatness of his headquarters can be improved
 D. how to express a suggestion which the maintainer plans to submit formally

23. Assume that you have determined that the work of one of your foremen and the men he supervises is consistently behind schedule. When you discuss this situation with the foreman, he tells you that his men are poor workers and then complains that he must spend all of his time checking on their work.
The following actions are offered for your consideration as possible ways of solving the problem of poor performance of the foreman and his men:
   I. Review the work standards with the foreman and determine whether they are realistic.
   II. Tell the foreman that you will recommend him for the foreman's training course for retraining.
   III. Ask the foreman for the names of the maintainers and then replace them as soon as possible.
   IV. Tell the foreman that you expect him to meet a satisfactory level of performance.
   V. Tell the foreman to insist that his men work overtime to catch up to the schedule.
   VI. Tell the foreman to review the type and amount of training he has given the maintainers.
   VII. Tell the foreman that he will be out of a job if he does not produce on schedule.
   VIII. Avoid all criticism of the foreman and his methods.
   Which of the following suggested answers CORRECTLY lists the proper actions to be taken to solve the problem of poor performance of the foreman and his men?
   A. I, II, IV, VI   B. I, III, V, VII   C. II, III, VI, VIII   D. IV, V, VI, VIII

23._____

24. When a conference or a group discussion is tending to turn into a *bull session* without constructive purpose, the BEST action to take is to
    A. reprimand the leader of the bull session
    B. redirect the discussion to the business at hand
    C. dismiss the meeting and reschedule it for another day
    D. allow the bull session to continue

24._____

25. Assume that you have been assigned responsibility for a program in which a high production rate is mandatory. From past experience, you know that your foremen do not perform equally well in the various types of jobs given to them. Which of the following methods should you use in selecting foremen for the specific types of work involved in the program?
    A. Leave the method of selecting foremen to your supervisor
    B. Assign each foreman to the work he does best
    C. Allow each foreman to choose his own job
    D. Assign each foreman to a job which will permit him to improve his own abilities

25._____

KEY (CORRECT ANSWERS)

1.	B	11.	C
2.	B	12.	D
3.	A	13.	B
4.	D	14.	B
5.	D	15.	C
6.	B	16.	D
7.	B	17.	C
8.	B	18.	B
9.	A	19.	A
10.	D	20.	B

21.	B
22.	A
23.	A
24.	B
25.	B

TEST 2

DIRECTIONS: Each question or incomplete statement is followed by several suggested answers or completions. Select the one that BEST answers the question or completes the statement. *PRINT THE LETTER OF THE CORRECT ANSWER IN THE SPACE AT THE RIGHT.*

1. A foreman who is familiar with modern management principles should know that the one of the following requirements of an administrator which is LEAST important is his ability to
   A. coordinate work
   B. plan, organize, and direct the work under his control
   C. cooperate with others
   D. perform the duties of the employees under his jurisdiction

2. When subordinates request his advice in solving problems encountered in their work, a certain chief occasionally answers the request by first asking the subordinate what he thinks should be done.
   This action by the chief is, on the whole,
   A. *desirable*, because it stimulates subordinates to give more thought to the solution of problems encountered
   B. *undesirable*, because it discourages subordinates from asking questions
   C. *desirable*, because it discourages subordinates from asking questions
   D. *undesirable*, because it undermines the confidence of subordinates in the ability of their supervisor

3. Of the following factors that may be considered by a unit head in dealing with the tardy subordinate, the one which should be given LEAST consideration is the
   A. frequency with which the employee is tardy
   B. effect of the employee's tardiness upon the work of other employees
   C. willingness of the employee to work overtime when necessary
   D. cause of the employee's tardiness

4. The MOST important requirement of a good inspectional report is that it should be
   A. properly addressed   B. lengthy
   C. clear and brief   D. spelled correctly

5. Building superintendents frequently inquire about departmental inspectional procedures.
   Of the following, it is BEST to
   A. advise them to write to the department for an official reply
   B. refuse as the inspectional procedure is a restricted matter
   C. briefly explain the procedure to them
   D. avoid the inquiry by changing the subject

6. Reprimanding a crew member before other workers is a
   A. *good* practice; the reprimand serves as a warning to the other workers
   B. *bad* practice; people usually resent criticism made in public
   C. *good* practice; the other workers will realize that the supervisor is fair
   D. *bad* practice; the other workers will take sides in the dispute

7. Of the following actions, the one which is LEAST likely to promote good work is for the group leader to
   A. praise workers for doing a good job
   B. call attention to the opportunities for promotion for better workers
   C. threaten to recommend discharge of workers who are below standard
   D. put into practice any good suggestion made by crew members

8. A supervisor notices that a member of his crew has skipped a routine step in his job.
   Of the following, the BEST action for the supervisor to take is to
   A. promptly question the worker about the incident
   B. immediately assign another man to complete the job
   C. bring up the incident the next time the worker asks for a favor
   D. say nothing about the incident but watch the worker carefully in the future

9. Assume you have been told to show a new worker how to operate a piece of equipment.
   Your FIRST step should be to
   A. ask the worker if he has any questions about the equipment
   B. permit the worker to operate the equipment himself while you carefully watch to prevent damage
   C. demonstrate the operation of the equipment for the worker
   D. have the worker read an instruction booklet on the maintenance of the equipment

10. Whenever a new man was assigned to his crew, the supervisor would introduce him to all other crew members, take him on a tour of the plant, tell him about bus schedules and places to eat.
    This practice is
    A. *good*; the new man is made to feel welcome
    B. *bad*; supervisors should not interfere in personal matters
    C. *good*; the new man knows that he can bring his personal problems to the supervisor
    D. *bad*; work time should not be spent on personal matters

11. The MOST important factor in successful leadership is the ability to
    A. obtain instant obedience to all orders
    B. establish friendly personal relations with crew members
    C. avoid disciplining crew members
    D. make crew members want to do what should be done

12. Explaining the reasons for departmental procedure to workers tends to
    A. waste time which should be used for productive purposes
    B. increase their interest in their work
    C. make them more critical of departmental procedures
    D. confuse them

13. If you want a job done well do it yourself.
    For a supervisor to follow this advice would be
    A. *good*; a supervisor is responsible for the work of his crew
    B. *bad*; a supervisor should train his men, not do their work
    C. *good*; a supervisor should be skilled in all jobs assigned to his crew
    D. *bad*; a supervisor loses respect when he works with his hands

14. When a supervisor discovers a mistake in one of the jobs for which his crew is responsible, it is MOST important for him to find out
    A. whether anybody else knows about the mistake
    B. who was to blame for the mistake
    C. how to prevent similar mistakes in the future
    D. whether similar mistakes occurred in the past

15. A supervisor who has to explain a new procedure to his crew should realize that questions from the crew USUALLY show that they
    A. are opposed to the new practice
    B. are completely confused by the explanation
    C. need more training in the new procedure
    D. are interested in the explanation

16. A good way for a supervisor to retain the confidence of his or her employees is to
    A. say as little as possible
    B. check work frequently
    C. make no promises unless they will be fulfilled
    D. never hesitate in giving an answer to any question

17. Good supervision is ESSENTIALLY a matter of
    A. patience in supervising workers
    B. care in selecting workers
    C. skill in human relations
    D. fairness in disciplining workers

18. It is MOST important for an employee who has been assigned a monotonous task to
    A. perform this task before doing other work
    B. ask another employee to help
    C. perform this task only after all other work has been completed
    D. take measures to prevent mistakes in performing the task

19. One of your employees has violated a minor agency regulation.
    The FIRST thing you should do is
    A. warn the employee that you will have to take disciplinary action if it should happen again
    B. ask the employee to explain his or her actions
    C. inform your supervisor and wait for advice
    D. write a memo describing the incident and place it in the employee's personnel file

20. One of your employees tells you that he feels you give him much more work than the other employees, and he is having trouble meeting your deadlines.
    You should
    A. ask if he has been under a lot of non-work related stress lately
    B. review his recent assignments to determine if he is correct
    C. explain that this is a busy time, but you are dividing the work equally
    D. tell him that he is the most competent employee and that is why he receives more work

21. A supervisor assigns one of his crew to complete a portion of a job. A short time later, the supervisor notices that the portion has not been completed.
    Of the following, the BEST way for the supervisor to handle this is to
    A. ask the crew member why he has not completed the assignment
    B. reprimand the crew member for not obeying orders
    C. assign another crew member to complete the assignment
    D. complete the assignment himself

22. Supposes that a member of your crew complains that you are *playing favorites* in assigning work.
    Of the following, the BEST method of handling the complaint is to
    A. deny it and refuse to discuss the matter with the worker
    B. take the opportunity to tell the worker what is wrong with his work
    C. ask the worker for examples to prove his point and try to clear up any misunderstanding
    D. promise to be more careful in making assignments in the future

23. A member of your crew comes to you with a complaint. After discussing the matter with him, it is clear that you have convinced him that his complaint was not justified.
    At this point, you should
    A. permit him to drop the matter
    B. make him admit his error
    C. pretend to see some justification in his complaint
    D. warn him against making unjustified complaints

24. Suppose that a supervisor has in his crew an older man who works rather slowly. In other respects, this man is a good worker; he is seldom absent, works carefully, never loafs, and is cooperative.

The BEST way for the supervisor to handle this worker is to
- A. try to get him to work faster and less carefully
- B. give him the most disagreeable job
- C. request that he be given special training
- D. permit him to work at his own speed

25. Suppose that a member of your crew comes to you with a suggestion he thinks will save time in doing a job. You realize immediately that it won't work.
Under these circumstances, your BEST action would be to
- A. thank the worker for the suggestion and forget about it
- B. explain to the worker why you think it won't work
- C. tell the worker to put the suggestion in writing
- D. ask the other members of your crew to criticize the suggestion

25.____

KEY (CORRECT ANSWERS)

1.	D	11.	D
2.	A	12.	B
3.	C	13.	B
4.	C	14.	C
5.	C	15.	D
6.	B	16.	C
7.	C	17.	C
8.	A	18.	D
9.	C	19.	B
10.	A	20.	B

21.	A
22.	C
23.	A
24.	D
25.	B

EXAMINATION SECTION
TEST 1

DIRECTIONS: Each question or incomplete statement is followed by several suggested answers or completions. Select the one that BEST answers the question or completes the statement. *PRINT THE LETTER OF THE CORRECT ANSWER IN THE SPACE AT THE RIGHT.*

1. Which one of the following is LEAST likely to be an area or cause of trouble in the use of staff personnel?

    A. Misunderstanding of the role the staff personnel are supposed to play as a result of vagueness of definition of their duties and authority
    B. Tendency of staff personnel almost always to be older than line personnel at comparable salary levels with whom they must deal
    C. Selection of staff personnel who fail to have simultaneously both competence in their specialities and skill in staff work
    D. The staff person fails to understand mixed staff and operating duties

1._____

2. Which of the following is generally NOT a valid statement with respect to the supervisory process?

    A. General supervision is more effective than close supervision.
    B. Employee-centered supervisors lead more effectively than do production-centered supervisors.
    C. Employee satisfaction is directly related to productivity.
    D. Low-producing supervisors use techniques that are different from high-producing supervisors.

2._____

3. Which of the following is the MOST essential element for proper evaluation of the performance of subordinate supervisors?

    A. Careful definition of each supervisor's specific job responsibilities and of his progress in meeting mutually agreed upon work goals
    B. System of rewards and penalties based on each supervisor's progress in meeting clearly defined performance standards
    C. Definition of personality traits, such as industry, initiative, dependability, and cooperativeness, required for effective job performance
    D. Breakdown of each supervisor's job into separate components and a rating of his performance on each individual task

3._____

4. The PRINCIPAL advantage of specialization for the operating efficiency of a public service agency is that specialization

    A. reduces the amount of red tape in coordinating the activities of mutually dependent departments
    B. simplifies the problem of developing adequate job controls
    C. provides employees with a clear understanding of the relationship of their activities to the overall objectives of the agency
    D. reduces destructive competition for power between departments

4._____

5. A list of conditions which encourages good morale inside a work group would NOT include a

   A. high rate of agreement among group members on values and objectives
   B. tight control system to minimize the risk of individual error
   C. good possibility that joint action will accomplish goals
   D. past history of successful group accomplishment

6. Of the following, the MOST important factor to be considered in selecting a training strategy or program is the

   A. requirements of the job to be performed by the trainees
   B. educational level or prior training of the trainees
   C. size of the training group
   D. quality and competence of available training specialists

7. Of the following, the one which is considered to be LEAST characteristic of the higher ranks of management is

   A. that higher levels of management benefit from modern technology
   B. that success is measured by the extent to which objectives are achieved
   C. the number of subordinates that directly report to a manager
   D. the de-emphasis of individual and specialized performance

8. Assume that a manager is preparing a training syllabus to be used in training members of her staff.
   Which of the following would NOT be a valid principle of the learning process to consider when preparing this training syllabus?

   A. When a person has thoroughly learned a task, it takes a lot of effort to create a little more improvement.
   B. In complicated learning situations, there is a period in which an additional period of practice produces an equal amount of improvement in learning.
   C. The less a person knows about the task, the slower the initial progress.
   D. The more a person knows about the task, the slower the initial progress.

9. Which statement BEST illustrates when collective bargaining agreements are working well?

   A. Executives strongly support subordinate managers.
   B. The management rights clause in the contract is clear and enforced.
   C. Contract provisions are competently interpreted.
   D. The provisions of the agreement are properly interpreted, communicated, and observed.

10. An executive who wishes to encourage subordinates to communicate freely with him about a job-related problem should FIRST

   A. state his own position on the problem before listening to the subordinates' ideas
   B. invite subordinates to give their own opinions on the problem
   C. ask subordinates for their reactions to his own ideas about the problem
   D. guard the confidentiality of management information about the problem

11. The ability to deal constructively with intra-organizational conflict is an essential attribute of the successful manager.
    The one of the following types of conflict which would be LEAST difficult to handle constructively is a situation in which there is

   A. agreement on objectives, but disagreement as to the probable results of adopting the various alternatives
   B. agreement on objectives, disagreement on alternative courses of action, and relative certainty as to the outcome of one of the alternatives
   C. disagreement on objectives and on alternative courses of action, and relative certainty as to the outcome of one of the alternatives
   D. disagreement on objectives and on alternative courses of action, but uncertainty as to the outcome of the alternatives

12. Which of the following actions does NOT belong in a properly conducted grievance handling process?

   A. Gathering relevant information on why the grievance arose
   B. Formulating a personal judgment about the fairness or unfairness of the grievance at the time the grievance is presented
   C. Establishing tentative answers to the grievance
   D. Following up to see whether the solution has eliminated the difficulty

13. Grievances are generally defined as complaints expressed over work-related matters.
    Which one of the following is MOST important for managers to be aware of in connection with this definition?
    The

   A. fact that the definition fails to separate the subject of the grievance from the attitude of the grievant
   B. fact that anything in the organization may be the source of the grievance
   C. need to assume that dissatisfied people have adverse effects on productivity
   D. implication that management should be concerned about expressed grievances and unconcerned about unexpressed grievances

14. In carrying out disciplinary action, the MOST important procedure for all managers to follow is to

    A. convince all levels of management on the need for discipline from the organization's viewpoint
    B. follow up on a disciplinary action and not assume that the action has been effective
    C. convince all executives that proper discipline is a legitimate tool for their use
    D. convince all executives that they need to display confidence in the organization's rules

15. Assume that an employee under your supervision is acquitted in court of criminal charges arising out of his employment.
    Of the following statements concerning disciplinary action, which is MOST NEARLY correct?

    A. Disciplinary proceedings against the employee may not be held for the same offenses on which he was tried and acquitted.
    B. In a disciplinary action, the acquittal dispenses with the requirement that the employee be advised as to his constitutional rights.
    C. Civil Rights Law Section 79 prohibits the taking of any further punitive action by an employer if the offense did not involve official corruption.
    D. It is possible for the employee to be found guilty of the same offense when tried in a departmental hearing.

16. Work rules can be an effective tool in the process of personnel management.
    The BEST practical definition for work rules is that they are

    A. minimum standards of conduct or performance that apply to individuals or groups at work in an organization
    B. prescriptions that serve to specialize employee behavior
    C. predetermined decisions about disciplinary action
    D. the major determinant of an organization's climate and the morale of its workforce

Questions 17-18

DIRECTIONS: Questions 17 and 18 pertain to identification of words that are incorrectly used because they are not in keeping with the meaning of the quotation. In answering each question, the first step is to read the passage and identify the incorrectly used word, and then select the word which, when substituted, BEST serves to convey the meaning of the quotation.

17. Among the Housing Manager's overall responsibilities in administering a project is the prevention of the development of conditions which might lead to termination of tenancy and eviction of a tenant. Where there appears to be doubt that a tenant is fully aware of his responsibilities and is thus jeopardizing his tenancy, the Housing Manager should acquaint him with these responsibilities. Where a situation involves behavior of a tenant or a member of his family, the Housing Manager should confirm, through discussions and referrals to social agencies, correction of the conditions before they reach a state where there is no alternative but termination proceedings.

17._____

   A. Coordinate
   B. Identify
   C. Assert
   D. Attempt

18. The one universal administrative complaint is that the budget is inadequate. Between adequacy and inadequacy lie all degrees of adequacy. Further, human wants are modest in relation to human resources. From these two facts we may conclude that the fundamental criterion of administrative decision must be a criterion of efficiency (the degree to which the goals have been reached relative to the available resources) rather than a criterion of adequacy (the degree to which its goals have been reached). The task of the manager is to maximize social values relative to limited resources.

18._____

   A. Improve
   B. Simple
   C. Limitless
   D. Optimize

Questions 19-21.

DIRECTIONS: Questions 19 through 21 are to be answered SOLELY on the basis of the following situation.

John Foley, a top administrator, is responsible for output in his organization. Because productivity had been lagging for two periods in a row, Foley decided to establish a committee of his subordinate managers to investigate the reasons for the poor performance and to make recommendations for improvements. After two meetings, the committee came to the conclusions and made the recommendations that follow.

Output forecasts had been handed down from the top without prior consultation with middle management and first level supervision. Lines of authority and responsibility had been unclear. The planning and control process should be decentralized.

After receiving the committee's recommendations, Foley proceeded to take the following actions. Foley decided he would retain final authority to establish quotas but would delegate to the middle managers the responsibility for meeting quotas.

After receiving Foley's decision, the middle managers proceeded to delegate to the first-line supervisors the authority to establish their own quotas. The middle managers eventually received and combined the first-line supervisors' quotas so that these conformed to Foley's.

19. Foley's decision to delegate responsibility for meeting quotas to the middle managers is inconsistent with sound management principles because

    A. Foley should not have involved himself in the first place
    B. middle managers do not have the necessary skills
    C. quotas should be established by the chief executive
    D. responsibility should not be delegated

19._____

20. The principle of co-extensiveness of responsibility and authority bears on Foley's decision.
    In this case, it implies that

    A. authority should exceed responsibility
    B. authority should be delegated to match the degree of responsibility
    C. both authority and responsibility should be retained and not delegated
    D. responsibility should be delegated, but authority should be retained

20._____

21. The middle managers' decision to delegate to the first-line supervisors the authority to establish quotas was INCORRECTLY reasoned because

    A. delegation and control must go together
    B. first-line supervisors are in no position to establish quotas
    C. one cannot delegate authority that one does not possess
    D. the meeting of quotas should not be delegated

21._____

22. If one attempts to list the advantages of the management-by-exception principle as it is used in connection with the budgeting process, several distinct advantages could be cited.
    Which of the following is NOT an advantage of this principle as it applies to the budgeting process?
    Management-by-exception

    A. saves time
    B. identifies critical problem areas
    C. focuses attention and concentrates effort
    D. escalates the frequency and importance of budget-related decisions

22._____

23. The MOST accurate description of a budget is that

    A. a budget is made up by an organization to plan its future activities
    B. a budget specifies in dollars and cents how much is spent in a particular time period
    C. a budget specifies how much the organization to which it relates estimates it will spend over a certain period of time
    D. all plans dealing with money are budgets

23._____

24. Of the following, the one which is NOT a contribution that a budget makes to organizational programming is that a budget   24._____

    A. enables a comparison of what actually happened with what was expected
    B. stresses the need to forecast specific goals and eliminates the need to focus on tasks needed to accomplish goals
    C. may illustrate duplication of effort between interdependent activities
    D. shows the relationship between various organizational segments

25. A line-item budget is a good control budget because   25._____

    A. it clearly specifies how the items being purchased will be used
    B. expenditures can be shown primarily for contractual services
    C. it clearly specifies what the money is buying
    D. it clearly specifies the services to be provided

KEY (CORRECT ANSWERS)

1.	B	11.	B
2.	C	12.	B
3.	A	13.	C
4.	B	14.	B
5.	B	15.	D
6.	A	16.	A
7.	A	17.	D
8.	D	18.	C
9.	D	19.	D
10.	B	20.	B

21. C
22. D
23. C
24. B
25. C

TEST 2

DIRECTIONS: Each question or incomplete statement is followed by several suggested answers or completions. Select the one that BEST answers the question or completes the statement. *PRINT THE LETTER OF THE CORRECT ANSWER IN THE SPACE AT THE RIGHT.*

1. The insights of Chester I. Barnard have influenced the development of management thought in significant ways. He is MOST closely identified with a position that has become known as the

    A. acceptance theory of authority
    B. principle of the manager's or executive's span of control
    C. *Theory X* and *Theory Y* dichotomy
    D. unit of command principle

    1._____

2. Certain conditions should exist to insure that a subordinate will decide to accept a communication as being authoritative.
Which of the following is LEAST valid as a condition which should exist?

    A. The subordinate understands the communication.
    B. At the time of the subordinate's decision, he views the communication as consistent with the organization's purpose and his personal interest.
    C. At the time of the subordinate's decision, he views the communication as more consistent with his personal purposes than with the organization's interest.
    D. The subordinate is mentally and physically able to comply with the communication.

    2._____

3. In exploring the effects that employee participation has on implementing changes in work methods, certain relationships have been established between participation and productivity.
It has MOST generally been found that highest productivity occurs in groups provided with

    A. participation in the process of change only through representatives of their group
    B. no participation in the change process
    C. full participation in the change process
    D. intermittent participation in the process of change

    3._____

4. The trend LEAST likely to occur in the area of employee-management relations is that

    A. employees will exert more influence on decisions affecting their interests
    B. technological change will have a stronger impact on organizations' human resources
    C. labor will judge management according to company profits
    D. government will play a larger role in balancing the interests of the parties in labor-management affairs

    4._____

5. Members of an organization must satisfy several fundamental psychological needs in order to be happy and productive.
The BROADEST and MOST basic needs are

   A. achievement, recognition, and acceptance
   B. competition, recognition, and accomplishment
   C. salary increments and recognition
   D. acceptance of competition and economic award

6. Morale has been defined as the capacity of a group of people to pull together steadily for a common purpose.
Morale thus defined is MOST generally dependent on

   A. job security
   B. group and individual self-confidence
   C. organizational efficiency
   D. physical health of the individuals

7. Which is the CORRECT order of steps to follow when revising office procedure?
To

   I. develop the improved method as determined by time and motion studies and effective workplace layout
   II. find out how the task is now performed
   III. apply the new method
   IV. analyze the current method

   The CORRECT answer is:
   A. IV, II, I, III
   B. II, I, III, IV
   C. I, II, IV, III
   D. II, IV, I, III

8. In contrast to broad spans of control, narrow spans of control are MOST likely to

   A. provide opportunity for more personal contact between superior and subordinate
   B. encourage decentralization
   C. stress individual initiative
   D. foster group of team effort

9. A manager is coaching a subordinate on the nature of decision-making. She could BEST define decision-making as

   A. choosing between alternatives
   B. making diagnoses of feasible ends
   C. making diagnoses of feasible means
   D. comparing alternatives

10. Of the following, the LEAST valid purpose of an organizational policy statement is to

    A. keep personnel from performing improper actions and functions on routine matters
    B. prevent the mishandling of non-routine matters
    C. provide management personnel with a tool that precludes the need for their use of judgment
    D. provide standard decisions and approaches in handling problems of a recurrent nature

11. Current thinking on bureaucratic organizations is that

    A. bureaucracy is on the way out
    B. bureaucracy, though not perfect, is unlikely to be replaced
    C. bureaucratic organizations are most effective in dealing with constant change
    D. bureaucratic organizations are most effective when dealing with sophisticated customers or clients

12. The development of alternate plans as a major step in planning will normally result in the planner's having several possible course of action available. GENERALLY, this is

    A. *desirable* since such development helps to determine the most suitable alternative and to provide for the unexpected
    B. *desirable* since such development makes the use of planning premises and constraints unnecessary
    C. *undesirable* since the planners should formulate only one way of achieving given goals at a given time
    D. *undesirable* since such action restricts efforts to modify the planning to take advantage of opportunities

13. Assume a manager carries out his responsibilities to his staff according to what is now known about managerial leadership.
    Which of the following statements would MOST accurately reflect his assumptions about proper management?

    A. Efficiency in operations results from allowing the human element to participate in a minimal way.
    B. Efficient operation results from balancing work considerations with personnel considerations.
    C. Efficient operation results from a work force committed to its self-interest.
    D. Efficient operation results from staff relationships that produce a friendly work climate.

14. Assume that a manager is called upon to conduct a management audit. To do this properly, he would have to take certain steps in a specific sequence. Which step should this manager take FIRST?

    A. Managerial performance must be surveyed.
    B. A method of reporting must be established.
    C. Management auditing procedures and documentation must be developed.
    D. Criteria for the audit must be established.

15. If a manager is required to conduct a scientific investigation of an organizational problem, the FIRST step he should take is to

    A. state his assumptions about the problem
    B. carry out a search for background information
    C. choose the right approach to investigate the validity of his assumptions
    D. define and state the problem

16. A manager would be correct to assert that the principle of delegation states that decisions should be made PRIMARILY

    A. by persons in an executive capacity qualified to make them
    B. by persons in a non-executive capacity
    C. at as low an organizational level of authority as practicable
    D. by the next lower level of authority

17. Of the following, which one is NOT regarded by management authorities as a fundamental characteristic of an ideal bureaucracy?

    A. Division of labor and specialization
    B. An established hierarchy
    C. Decentralization of authority
    D. A set of operating rules and regulations

18. As the number of subordinates in a manager's span of control increases, the actual number of possible relationships

    A. increases disproportionately to the number of subordinates
    B. increases in equal number to the number of subordinates
    C. reaches a stable level
    D. will first increase, then slowly decrease

19. Management experts generally believe that computer-based management information systems (MIS) have greater potential for improving the process of management than any other development in recent decades.
The one of the following which MOST accurately describes the objectives of MIS is to

    A. provide information for decision-making on planning, initiating, and controlling the operations of the various units of the organization
    B. establish mechanization of routine functions such as clerical records, payroll, inventory, and accounts receivable in order to promote economy and efficiency
    C. computerize decision-making on planning, initiating, organizing, and controlling the operations of an organization
    D. provide accurate facts and figures on the various programs of the organization to be used for purposes of planning and research

20. The one of the following which is the BEST application of the *management-by-exception* principle is that this principle

    A. stimulates communication and aids in management of crisis situations, thus reducing the frequency of decision-making
    B. saves time and reserves top management decisions only for crisis situations, thus reducing the frequency of decision-making
    C. stimulates communication, saves time, and reduces the frequency of decision-making
    D. is limited to crisis-management situations

21. Generally, each organization is dependent upon the availability of qualified personnel.
Of the following, the MOST important factor affecting the availability of qualified people to each organization is

    A. availability of public transportation
    B. the general rise in the educational levels of our population
    C. the rise of sentiment against racial discrimination
    D. pressure by organized community groups

22. A fundamental responsibility of all managers is to decide what physical facilities and equipment are needed to help attain basic goals.
Good planning for the purchase and use of equipment is seldom easy to do and is complicated most by the fact that

    A. organizations rarely have stable sources of supply
    B. nearly all managers tend to be better at personnel planning than at equipment planning
    C. decisions concerning physical resources are made too often on an emergency basis rather than under carefully prepared policies
    D. legal rulings relative to depreciation fluctuate very frequently

23. In attempting to reconcile managerial objectives and an individual employee's goals, it is generally LEAST desirable for management to

    A. recognize the capacity of the individual to contribute toward realization of managerial goals
    B. encourage self-development of the employee to exceed minimum job performance
    C. consider an individual employee's work separately from other employees
    D. demonstrate that an employee advances only to the extent that he contributes directly to the accomplishment of stated goals

24. As a management tool for discovering individual training needs, a job analysis would generally be of LEAST assistance in determining

    A. the performance requirements of individual jobs
    B. actual employee performance on the job
    C. acceptable standards of performance
    D. training needs for individual jobs

25. One of the major concerns of organizational managers today is how the spread of automation will affect them and the status of their positions. Realistically speaking, one can say that the MOST likely effect of our newer forms of highly automated technology on managers will be to

    A. make most top-level positions superfluous or obsolete
    B. reduce the importance of managerial work in general
    C. replace the work of managers with the work of technicians
    D. increase the importance of and demand for top managerial personnel

KEY (CORRECT ANSWERS)

1.	A	11.	B
2.	C	12.	A
3.	C	13.	B
4.	C	14.	D
5.	A	15.	D
6.	B	16.	C
7.	D	17.	C
8.	A	18.	A
9.	A	19.	A
10.	C	20.	C

21. B
22. C
23. C
24. B
25. D

PREPARING WRITTEN MATERIAL

PARAGRAPH REARRANGEMENT
COMMENTARY

The sentences that follow are in scrambled order. You are to rearrange them in proper order and indicate the letter choice containing the correct answer at the space at the right.

Each group of sentences in this section is actually a paragraph presented in scrambled order. Each sentence in the group has a place in that paragraph; no sentence is to be left out. You are to read each group of sentences and decide upon the best order in which to put the sentences so as to form a well-organized paragraph.

The questions in this section measure the ability to solve a problem when all the facts relevant to its solution are not given.

More specifically, certain positions of responsibility and authority require the employee to discover connection between events sometimes, apparently, unrelated. In order to do this, the employee will find it necessary to correctly infer that unspecified events have probably occurred or are likely to occur. This ability becomes especially important when action must be taken on incomplete information.

Accordingly, these questions require competitors to choose among several suggested alternatives, each of which presents a different sequential arrangement of the events. Competitors must choose the MOST logical of the suggested sequences.

In order to do so, they may be required to draw on general knowledge to infer missing concepts or events that are essential to sequencing the given events. Competitors should be careful to infer only what is essential to the sequence. The plausibility of the wrong alternatives will always require the inclusion of unlikely events or of additional chains of events which are NOT essential to sequencing the given events.

It's very important to remember that you are looking for the best of the four possible choices, and that the best choice of all may not even be one of the answers you're given to choose from.

There is no one right way to solve these problems. Many people have found it helpful to first write out the order of the sentences, as they would have arranged them, on their scrap paper before looking at the possible answers. If their optimum answer is there, this can save them some time. If it isn't, this method can still give insight into solving the problem. Others find it most helpful to just go through each of the possible choices, contrasting each as they go along. You should use whatever method feels comfortable and works for you.

While most of these types of questions are not that difficult, we've added a higher percentage of the difficult type, just to give you more practice. Usually there are only one or two questions on this section that contain such subtle distinctions that you're unable to answer confidently. And you then may find yourself stuck deciding between two possible choices, neither of which you're sure about.

EXAMINATION SECTION
TEST 1

DIRECTIONS: The sentences that follow are in scrambled order. You are to rearrange them in proper order and indicate the letter choice containing the correct answer. *PRINT THE LETTER OF THE CORRECT ANSWER IN THE SPACE AT THE RIGHT.*

1. Below are four statements labeled W, X, Y and Z. 1.____
   W. He was a strict and fanatic drillmaster.
   X. The word is always used in a derogatory sense and generally shows resentment and anger on the part of the user.
   Y. It is from the name of this Frenchman that we derive our English word, martinet.
   Z. Jean Martinet was the Inspector-General of Infantry during the reign of King Louis XIV.
   The PROPER order in which these sentences should be placed in a paragraph is:
   A. X, Z, W, Y   B. X, Z, Y, W   C. Z, W, Y, X   D. Z, Y, W, X

2. In the following paragraph, the sentences, which are numbered, have been jumbled. 2.____
   I. Since then it has undergone changes.
   II. It was incorporated in 1955 under the laws of the State of New York.
   III. Its primary purposes, a cleaner city, has, however, remained the same.
   IV. The Citizens Committee works in cooperation with the Mayor's Inter- 3.____
   departmental Committee for a Clean City.
   The order in which these sentences should be arranged to form a well-organized paragraph is:
   A. II, IV, I, III   B. III, IV, I, II   C. IV, II, I, III   D. IV, III, II, I

Questions 3-5.

DIRECTIONS: The sentences listed below are part of a meaningful paragraph but they are not given in their proper order. You are to decide what would be the BEST order in which to put the sentences so as to form a well-organized paragraph. Each sentence has a place in the paragraph; there are no extra sentences. You are then to answer Questions 3 through 5 inclusive on the basis of your rearrangements of these scrambled sentences into a properly organized paragraph.

In 1887 some insurance companies organized an Inspection Department to advise their clients on all phases of fire prevention and protection. Probably this has been due to the smaller annual fire losses in Great Britain than in the United States. It tests various fire prevention devices and appliances and determines manufacturing hazards and their safeguards. Fire research began earlier in the United States and is more advanced than in Great Britain. Later they established a laboratory specializing in electrical, mechanical, hydraulic, and chemical fields.

3. When the five sentences are arranged in proper order, the paragraph starts with the sentence which begins
   A. "In 1887..." B. "Probably this..." C. "It tests..."
   D. "Fire research..." E. "Later they..."

4. In the last sentence listed above, "they" refers to
   A. the insurance companies
   B. the United States and Great Britain
   C. the Inspection Department
   D. clients
   E. technicians

5. When the above paragraph is properly arranged, it ends with the words
   A. "...and protection."
   B. "...the United States."
   C. "...their safeguards."
   D. "...in Great Britain."
   E. "...chemical fields."

KEY (CORRECT ANSWERS)

1. C
2. C
3. D
4. A
5. C

TEST 2

DIRECTIONS: In each of the questions numbered I through V, several sentences are given. For each question, choose as your answer the group of number that represents the MOST logical order of these sentences if they were arranged in paragraph form. *PRINT THE LETTER OF THE CORRECT ANSWER IN THE SPACE AT THE RIGHT.*

1. I. It is established when one shows that the landlord has prevented the tenant's enjoyment of his interest in the property leased.
    II. Constructive eviction is the result of a breach of the covenant of quiet enjoyment implied in all leases.
    III. In some parts of the United States, it is not complete until the tenant vacates within a reasonable time.
    IV. Generally, the acts must be of such serious and permanent character as to deny the tenant the enjoyment of his possessing rights.
    V. In this event, upon abandonment of the premises, the tenant's liability for that ceases.
    The CORRECT answer is:
    A. II, I, IV, III, V
    B. V, II, III, I, IV
    C. IV, III, I, II, V
    D. I, III, V, IV, II

    1.____

2. I. The powerlessness before private and public authorities that is the typical experience of the slum tenant is reminiscent of the situation of blue-collar workers all through the nineteenth century.
    II. Similarly, in recent years, this chapter of history has been reopened by anti-poverty groups which have attempted to organize slum tenants to enable them to bargain collectively with their landlords about the conditions of their tenancies.
    III. It is familiar history that many of the worker remedied their condition by joining together and presenting their demands collectively.
    IV. Like the workers, tenants are forced by the conditions of modern life into substantial dependence on these who possess great political aid and economic power.
    V. What's more, the very fact of dependence coupled with an absence of education and self-confidence makes them hesitant and unable to stand up for what they need from those in power.
    The CORRECT answer is:
    A. V, IV, I, II, III
    B. II, III, I, V, IV
    C. III, I, V, IV, II
    D. I, IV, V, III, II

    2.____

3. I. A railroad, for example, when not acting as a common carrier may contract away responsibility for its own negligence.
    II. As to a landlord, however, no decision has been found relating to the legal effect of a clause shifting the statutory duty of repair to the tenant.
    III. The courts have not passed on the validity of clauses relieving the landlord of this duty and liability.
    IV. They have, however, upheld the validity of exculpatory clauses in other types of contracts.

    3.____

V. Housing regulations impose a duty upon the landlord to maintain leased premises in safe condition.
VI. As another example, a bailee may limit his liability except for gross negligence, willful acts, or fraud.

The CORRECT answer is:
A. II, I, VI, IV, III, V
B. I, III, IV, V, VI, II
C. III, V, I, IV, II, VI
D. V, III, IV, I, VI, II

4.
I. Since there are only samples in the building, retail or consumer sales are generally eschewed by mart occupants, and in some instances, rigid controls are maintained to limit entrance to the mart only to those persons engaged in retailing.
II. Since World War I, in many larger cities, there has developed a new type of property, called the mart building.
III. It can, therefore, be used by wholesalers and jobbers for the display of sample merchandise.
IV. This type of building is most frequently a multi-storied, finished interior property which is a cross between a retail arcade and a loft building.
V. This limitation enables the mart occupants to ship the orders from another location after the retailer or dealer makes his selection from the samples.

The CORRECT answer is:
A. II, IV, III, I, V
B. IV, III, V, I, II
C. I, III, II, IV, V
D. I, IV, II, III, V

5.
I. In general, staff-line friction reduces the distinctive contribution of staff personnel.
II. The conflicts, however, introduce an uncontrolled element into the managerial system.
III. On the other hand, the natural resistance of the line to staff innovations probably usefully restrains over-eager efforts to apply untested procedures on a large scale.
IV. Under such conditions, it is difficult to know when valuable ideas are being sacrificed.
V. The relatively weak position of staff, requiring accommodation to the line, tends to restrict their ability to engage in free, experimental innovation.

The CORRECT answer is:
A. IV, II, III, I, V
B. I, V, III, II, IV
C. V, III, I, II, IV
D. II, I, IV, V, III

KEY (CORRECT ANSWERS)

1. A
2. D
3. D
4. A
5. B

TEST 3

DIRECTIONS: Questions 1 through 4 consist of six sentences which can be arranged in a logical sequence. For each question, select the choice which places the numbered sentences in the MOST logical sequent. *PRINT THE LETTER OF THE CORRECT ANSWER IN THE SPACE AT THE RIGHT.*

1. I. The burden of proof as to each issue is determined before trial and remains upon the same party throughout the trial.
    II. The jury is at liberty to believe one witness' testimony as against a number of contradictory witnesses.
    III. In a civil case, the party bearing the burden of proof is required to prove his contention by a fair preponderance of the evidence.
    IV. However, it must be noted that a fair preponderance of evidence does not necessarily mean a greater number of witnesses.
    V. The burden of proof is the burden which rests upon one of the parties to an action to persuade the trier of the facts, generally the jury, that a proposition he asserts is true.
    VI. If the evidence is equally balanced, or if it leaves the jury in such doubt as to be unable to decide the controversy either way, judgment must be given against the party upon whom the burden of proof rests.
    The CORRECT answer is:
    A. III, II, V, IV, I, VI
    B. I, II, VI, V, III, IV
    C. III, IV, V, I, II, VI
    D. V, I, III, VI, IV, II

1.____

2. I. If a parent is without assets and is unemployed, he cannot be convicted of the crime of non-support of a child.
    II. The term "sufficient ability" has been held to mean sufficient financial ability.
    III. It does not matter if his unemployment is by choice or unavoidable circumstances.
    IV. If he fails to take any steps at all, he may be liable to prosecution for endangering the welfare of a child.
    V. Under the penal law, a parent is responsible for the support of his minor child only if the parent is "of sufficient ability."
    VI. An indigent parent may meet his obligation by borrowing money or by seeking aid under the provisions of the Social Welfare Law.
    The CORRECT answer is:
    A. VI, I, V, III, II, IV
    B. I, III, V, II, IV, VI
    C. V, II, I, III, VI, IV
    D. I, VI, IV, V, II, III

2.____

3. I. Consider, for example, the case of a rabble rouser who urges a group of twenty people to go out and break the windows of a nearby factory.
    II. Therefore, the law fills the indicated gap with the crime of inciting to riot.
    III. A person is considered guilty of inciting to riot when he urges ten or more persons to engage in tumultuous and violent conduct of a kind likely to create public alarm.
    IV. However, if he has not obtained the cooperation of at least four people, he cannot be charged with unlawful assembly.

3.____

143

V. The charge of inciting to riot was added to the law to cover types of conduct which cannot be classified as either the crime of "riot" or the crime of "unlawful assembly."
VI. If he acquires the acquiescence of at least four of them, he is guilty of unlawful assembly even if the project does not materialize.

The CORRECT answer is:
  A. III, V, I, VI, IV, II
  B. V, I, IV, VI, II, III
  C. III, IV, I, V, II, VI
  D. V, I, IV, VI, III, II

4. I. If, however, the rebuttal evidence presents an issue of credibility, it is for the jury to determine whether the presumption has, in fact, been destroyed.
    II. Once sufficient evidence to the contrary is introduced, the presumption disappears from the trial.
    III. The effect of a presumption is to place the burden upon the adversary to come forward with evidence to rebut the presumption.
    IV. When a presumption is overcome and ceases to exist in the case, the fact or facts which gave rise to the presumption still remain.
    V. Whether a presumption has been overcome is ordinarily a question for the court.
    VI. Such information may furnish a basis for a logical inference.

The CORRECT answer is:
  A. IV, VI, II, V, I, III
  B. III, II, V, I, IV, VI
  C. V, III, VI, IV, II, I
  D. V, IV, I, II, VI, III

KEY (CORRECT ANSWERS)

1. D
2. C
3. A
4. B

SUPERVISION STUDY GUIDE

Social science has developed information about groups and leadership in general and supervisor-employee relationships in particular. Since organizational effectiveness is closely linked to the ability of supervisors to direct the activities of employees, these findings are important to executives everywhere.

IS A SUPERVISOR A LEADER?

First-line supervisors are found in all large business and government organizations. They are the men at the base of an organizational hierarchy. Decisions made by the head of the organization reach them through a network of intermediate positions. They are frequently referred to as part of the management team, but their duties seldom seem to support this description.

A supervisor of clerks, tax collectors, meat inspectors, or securities analysts is not charged with budget preparation. He cannot hire or fire the employees in his own unit on his say-so. He does not administer programs which require great planning, coordinating, or decision making.

Then what is he? He is the man who is directly in charge of a group of employees doing productive work for a business or government agency. If the work requires the use of machines, the men he supervises operate them. If the work requires the writing of reports, the men he supervises write them. He is expected to maintain a productive flow of work without creating problems which higher levels of management must solve. But is he a leader?

To carry out a specific part of an agency's mission, management creates a unit, staffs it with a group of employees and designates a supervisor to take charge of them. Management directs what this unit shall do, from time to time changes directions, and often indicates what the group should not do. Management presumably creates status for the supervisor by giving him more pay, a title, and special privileges.

Management asks a supervisor to get his workers to attain organizational goals, including the desired quantity and quality of production. Supposedly, he has authority to enable him to achieve this objective. Management at least assumes that by establishing the status of the supervisor's position, it has created sufficient authority to enable him to achieve these goals— not his goals, nor necessarily the group's, but management's goals.

In addition, supervision includes writing reports, keeping records of membership in a higher-level administrative group, industrial engineering, safety engineering, editorial duties, housekeeping duties, etc. The supervisor as a member of an organizational network, must be responsible to the changing demands of the management above him. At the same time, he must be responsive to the demands of the work group of which he is a member. He is placed in the difficult position of communicating and implementing new decisions, changed programs and revised production quotas for his work group, although he may have had little part in developing them.

It follows, then, that supervision has a special characteristic: achievement of goals, previously set by management, through the efforts of others. It is in this feature of the supervisor's job that we find the role of a leader in the sense of the following definition: *A leader is that person who most effectively influences group activities toward goal setting and goal achievements.*

This definition is broad. It covers both leaders in groups that come together voluntarily and in those brought together through a work assignment in a factory, store, or government agency. In the natural group, the authority necessary to attain goals is determined by the group membership and is granted by them. In the working group, it is apparent that the establishment of a supervisory position creates a predisposition on the part of employees to accept the authority of the occupant of that position. We cannot, however, assume that mere occupation confers authority sufficient to assure the accomplishment of an organization's goals.

Supervision is different, then, from leadership. The supervisor is expected to fulfill the role of leader but without obtaining a grant of authority from the group he supervises. The supervisor is expected to influence the group in the achieving of goals but is often handicapped by having little influence on the organizational process by which goals are set. The supervisor, because he works in an organizational setting, has the burdens of additional organizational duties and restrictions and requirements arising out of the fact that his position is subordinate to a hierarchy of higher-level supervisors. These differences between leadership and supervision are reflected in our definition: *Supervision is basically a leadership role, in a formal organization, which has as its objective the effective influencing of other employees.*

Even though these differences between supervision and leadership exist, a significant finding of experimenters in this field is that supervisors must be leaders to be successful.

The problem is: How can a supervisor exercise leadership in an organizational setting? We might say that the supervisor is expected to be a natural leader in a situation which does not come about naturally. His situation becomes really difficult in an organization which is more eager to make its supervisors into followers rather than leaders.

LEADERSHIP: NATURAL AND ORGANIZATIONAL

Leadership, in its usual sense of *natural* leadership, and supervision are not the same. In some cases, leadership embraces broader powers and functions than supervision; in other cases, supervision embraces more than leadership. This is true both because of the organization and technical aspects of the supervisor's job and because of the relatively freer setting and inherent authority of the natural leader.

The natural leader usually has much more authority and influence than the supervisor. Group members not only follow his command but prefer it that way. The employee, however, can appeal the supervisor's commands to his union or to the supervisor's superior or to the personnel office. These intercessors represent restrictions on the supervisor's power to lead.

The natural leader can gain greater membership involvement in the group's objectives, and he can change the objectives of the group. The supervisor can attempt to gain employee support only for management's objectives; he cannot set other objectives. In these instances leadership is broader than supervision.

The natural leader must depend upon whatever skills are available when seeking to attain objectives. The supervisor is trained in the administrative skills necessary to achieve management's goals. If he does not possess the requisite skills, however, he can call upon management's technicians.

A natural leader can maintain his leadership, in certain groups, merely by satisfying members' need for group affiliation. The supervisor must maintain his leadership by directing and organizing his group to achieve specific organizational goals set for him and his group by management. He must have a technical competence and a kind of coordinating ability which is not needed by many natural leaders.

A natural leader is responsible only to his group which grants him authority. The supervisor is responsible to management, which employs him, and also to the work group of which he is a member. The supervisor has the exceedingly difficult job of reconciling the demands of two groups frequently in conflict. He is often placed in the untenable position of trying to play two antagonistic roles. In the above instance, supervision is broader than leadership.

ORGANIZATIONAL INFLUENCES ON LEADERSHIP

The supervisor is both a product and a prisoner of the organization wherein we find him. The organization which creates the supervisor's position also obstructs, restricts, and channelizes the exercise of his duties. These influences extend beyond prescribed functional relationships to specific supervisory behavior. For example, even in a face-to-face situation involving one of his subordinates, the supervisor's actions are controlled to a great extent by his organization. His behavior must conform to the organization policy on human relations, rules which dictate personnel procedures, specific prohibitions governing conduct, the attitudes of his own superior, etc. He is not a free agent operating within the limits of his work group. His freedom of action is much more circumscribed than is generally admitted. The organizational influences which limit his leadership actions can be classified as structure, prescriptions, and proscriptions.

The organizational structure places each supervisor's position in context with other designated positions. It determines the relationships between his position and specific positions which impinge on his. The structure of the organization designates a certain position to which he looks for orders and information about his work. It gives a particular status to his position within a pattern of statuses from which he perceives that (1) certain positions are on a par, organizationally, with his, (2) other positions are subordinate, and (3) still others are superior.

The organizational structure determines those positions to which he should look for advice and assistance, and those positions to which he should give advice and assistance.

For instance, the organizational structure has predetermined that the supervisor of a clerical processing unit shall report to a supervisory position in a higher echelon. He shall have certain relationships with the supervisors of the work units which transmit work to and receive work from his unit. He shall discuss changes and clarification of procedures with certain staff units, such as organization and methods, cost accounting, and personnel. He shall consult supervisors of units which provide or receive special work assignments.

The organizational structure, however, establishes patterns other than those of the relationships of positions. These are the patterns of responsibility, authority, and expectations.

The supervisor is responsible for certain activities or results; he is presumably invested with the authority to achieve these. His set of authority and responsibility is interwoven with other sets to the end that all goals and functions of the organization are parceled out in small, manageable lots. This, of course, establishes a series of expectations: a single supervisor can perform his particular set of duties only upon the assumption that preceding or contiguous sets of duties have been, or are being carried out. At the same time, he is aware of the expectations of others that he will fulfill his functional role.

The structure of an organization establishes relationships between specified positions and specific expectations for these positions. The fact that these relationships and expectations are established is one thing; whether or not they are met is another.

PRESCRIPTIONS AND PROSCRIPTIONS

But let us return to the organizational influences which act to restrict the supervisor's exercise of leadership. These are the prescriptions and proscriptions generally in effect in all organizations, and those peculiar to a single organization. In brief these are the *thou shalt's* and the *thou shalt not's*.

Organizations not only prescribe certain duties for individual supervisory positions, they also prescribe specific methods and means of carrying out these duties and maintaining management-employee relations. These include rules, regulations, policy, and tradition. It does no good for the supervisor to say, *This seems to be the best way to handle such-and-such,* if the organization has established a routine for dealing with problems. For good or bad, there are rules that state that firings shall be executed in such a manner, accompanied by a certain notification; that training shall be conducted, and in this manner. Proscriptions are merely negative prescriptions; you may not discriminate against any employee because of politics or race; you shall not suspend any employee without following certain procedures and obtaining certain approvals.

Most of these prohibitions and rules apply to the area of interpersonal relations, precisely the area which is now arousing most interest on the part of administrators and managers. We have become concerned about the contrast between formally prescribed relationships and interpersonal relationships, and this brings us to the often discussed informal organization.

FORMAL AND INFORMAL ORGANIZATIONS

As we well know, the functions and activities of any organization are broken down into individual units of work called positions. Administrators must establish a pattern which will link these positions to each other and relate them to a system of authority and responsibility. Man-to-man are spelled out as plainly as possible for all to understand. Managers, then, build an official structure which we call the formal organization.

In these same organizations, employees react individually and in groups to institutionally determined roles. John, a worker, rides in the same carpool as Joe, a foreman. An unplanned communication develops. Harry, a machinist knows more about high-speed machining than his foreman or anyone else in his shop. An unofficial tool boss comes into being. Mary, who fought with Jane, is promoted over her. Jane now gives Mary's directions. A planned relationship fails to develop. The employees have built a structure which we call the informal organization.

Formal organization is a system of management-prescribed relations between positions in an organization.

Informal organization is a network of unofficial relations between people in an organization.

These definitions might lead us to the absurd conclusion that positions carry out formal activities and that employe4es spend their time in unofficial activities. We must recognize that organizational activities are in all cases carried out by people. The formal structure provides a needed framework within which interpersonal relations occur. What we call informal organization is the complex of normal, natural relations among employees. These personal relationships may be negative or positive. That is, they may impede or aid the achievement of organizational goals. For example, friendship between two supervisors greatly increases the probability of good cooperation and coordination between their sections. On the other hand, *buck passing* nullifies the formal structure by failure to meet a prescribed and expected responsibility.

It is improbable that an ideal organization exists where all activities are carried out in strict conformity to a formally prescribed pattern of functional roles. Informal organization arises because of the incompleteness and ambiguities in the network of formally prescribed relationships, or in response to the needs or inadequacies of supervisors or managers who hold prescribed functional roles in an organization. Many of these relationships are not prescribed by the organizational pattern; many cannot be prescribed; many should not be prescribed.

Management faces the problem of keeping the informal organization in harmony with the mission of the agency. One way to do this is to make sure that all employees have a clear understanding of and are sympathetic with that mission. The issuance of organizational charts, procedural manuals, and functional descriptions of the work to be done by divisions and sections helps communicate management's plans and goals. Issuances alone, of course, cannot do the whole job. They should be accompanied by oral discussion and explanation. Management must ensure that there is mutual understanding and acceptance of charts and procedures. More important is that management acquaint itself with the attitudes, activities, and peculiar brands of logic which govern the informal organization. Only through this type of knowledge can they and supervisors keep informal goals consistent with the agency mission.

SUPERVISION STATUS AND FUNCTIONAL ROLE

A well-established supervisor is respected by the employees who work with him. They defer to his wishes. It is clear that a superior-subordinate relationship has been established. That is, status of the supervisor has been established in relation to other employees of the same work group. This same supervisor gains the respect of employees when he behaves in as certain manner. He will be expected, generally, to follow the customs of the group in such matters as dress, recreation, and manner of speaking. The group has a set of expectations as to his behavior. His position is a functional role which carries with it a collection of rights and obligations.

The position of supervisor usually has a status distinct from the individual who occupies it: it is much like a position description which exists whether or not there is an incumbent. The status of a supervisory position is valued higher than that of an employee position both because of the functional role of leadership which is assigned to it and because of the status symbols of titles, rights, and privileges which go with it.

Social ranking, or status, is not simple because it involves both the position and the man. An individual may be ranked higher than others because of his education, social background, perceived leadership ability, or conformity to group customs and ideals. If such a man is ranked higher by the members of a work group than their supervisor, the supervisor's effectiveness may be seriously undermined.

If the organization does not build and reinforce a supervisor's status, his position can be undermined in a different way. This will happen when managers go around rather than through the supervisor or designate him as a straw boss, acting boss, or otherwise not a real boss.

Let us clarify this last point. A role, and corresponding status, establishes a set of expectations. Employees expect their supervisor to do certain things and to act in certain ways. They are prepared to respond to that expected behavior. When the supervisor's behavior does not conform to their expectations, they are surprised, confused, and ill-at-ease. It becomes necessary for them to resolve their confusion, if they can. They might do this by turning to one of their own members for leadership. If the confusion continues, or their attempted solutions are not satisfactory, they will probably become a poorly motivated, non-cohesive group which cannot function very well.

COMMUNICATION AND THE SUPERVISOR

In a recent survey, railroad workers reported that they rarely look to their supervisor for information about the company. This is startling, at least to us, because we ordinarily think of the supervisor as the link between management and worker. We expect the supervisor to be the prime source of information about the company. Actually, the railroad workers listed the supervisor next to last in the o5rder of their sources of information. Most surprising of all, the supervisors, themselves, stated that rumor and unofficial contacts were their principal sources of information. Here we see one of the reasons why supervisors may not be as effective as management desires.

The supervisor is not only being bypassed by his work group, he is being ignored, and his position weakened, by the very organization which is holding him responsible for the activities of his workers. If he is management's representative to the employee, then management has an obligation to keep him informed of its activities. This is necessary if he is to carry out his functions efficiently and maintain his leadership in the work group. The supervisor is expected to be a source of information; when he is not, his status is not clear, and employees are dissatisfied because he has not lived up to expectations.

By providing information to the supervisor to pass along to employees, we can strengthen his position as leader of the group, and increase satisfaction and cohesion within the group. Because he has more information than the other members, receives information sooner, and passes it along at the proper times, members turn to him as a source and also provide him with information in the hope of receiving some in return. From this, we can see an increase in group cohesiveness because:

- Employees are bound closer to their supervisor because he is *in the know*.
- There is less need to go outside the group for answers
- Employees will more quickly turn to the supervisor for enlightenment

The fact that he has the answers will also enhance the supervisor's standing in the eyes of his men. This increased status will serve to bolster his authority and control of the group and will probably result in improved morale and productivity.

The foregoing, of course, does not mean that all management information should be given out. There are obviously certain policy determinations and discussions which need not or cannot be transmitted to all supervisors. However, the supervisor must be kept as fully informed as possible so that he can answer questions when asked and can allay needless fears and anxieties. Further, the supervisor has the responsibility of encouraging employee questions and submissions of information. He must be able to present information to employees so that it is clearly understood and accepted. His attitude and manner should make it clear that he believes in what he is saying, that the information is necessary or desirable to the group, and that he is prepared to act on the basis of the information.

SUPERVISION AND JOB PERFORMANCE

The productivity of work groups is a product; employees' efforts are multiplied by the supervision they receive. Many investigators have analyzed this relationship and have discovered elements of supervision which differentiate high and low production groups. These researchers have identified certain types of supervisory practices which they classify as *employee-centered* and other types which they classify as *production centered*.

The difference between these two kinds of supervision lies not in specific practices but in the approach or orientation to supervision. The employee-centered supervisor directs most of his efforts toward increasing employee motivation. He is concerned more with realizing the potential energy of persons than with administrative and technological methods of increasing efficiency and productivity. He is the man who finds ways of causing employees to want to work harder with the same tools. These supervisors emphasize the personal relations between their employees and themselves.

Now, obviously, these pictures are overdrawn. No one supervisor has all the virtues of the ideal type of employee-centered supervisor. And, fortunately, no one supervisor has all the bad traits found in many production-centered supervisors. We should remember that the various practices that researchers have fond which distinguish these two kinds of supervision represent the many practices and methods of supervisors of all gradations between these extremes. We should be careful, too, of the implications of the labels attached to the two types. For instance, being production-centered is not necessarily bad, since the principal responsibility of any supervisor is maintaining the production level that is expected of his work group. Being employee-centered may not necessarily be good, if the only result is a happy, chuckling crew of loafers. To return to the researchers' findings, employee-centered supervisors:

- Recommend promotions, transfers, pay increases
- Inform men about what is happening in the company
- Keep men posted on how well they are doing
- Hear complaints and grievances sympathetically
- Speak up for subordinates

Production-centered supervisors, on the other hand, don't do those things. They check on employees more frequently, give more detailed and frequent instructions, don't give reasons for changes, and are more punitive when mistakes are made. Employee-centered supervisors were reported to contribute to high morale and high production, whereas production-centered supervision was associated with lower morale and less production.

More recent findings, however, show that the relationship between supervision and productivity is not this simple. Investigators now report that high production is more frequently associated with supervisory practices which combine employee-centered behavior with concern for production. (This concern is not the same, however, as anxiety about production, which is the hallmark of our production-centered supervisor.) Let us examine these apparently contradictory findings and the premises from which they are derived.

SUPERVISION AND MORALE

Why do supervisory activities cause high or low production? As the name implies, the activities of the employee-centered supervisor tend to relate him more closely and satisfactorily to his workers. The production-centered supervisor's practices tend to separate him from his group and to foster antagonism. An analysis of this difference may answer our question.

Earlier, we pointed out that the supervisor is a type of leader and that leadership is intimately related to the group in which it occurs We discover, now, that an employee-centered supervisor's primary activities are concerned with both his leadership and his group membership. Such a supervisor is a member of a group and occupies a leadership role in that group.

These facts are sometimes obscured when we speak of the supervisor as management's representative, or as the organizational link between management and the employee, or as the end of the chain of command. If we really want to understand what it is we expect of the supervisor, we must remember that he is the designated leader of a group of employees to whom he is bound by interaction and interdependence.

Most of his actions are aimed, consciously or unconsciously, at strengthening membership ties in the group. This includes both making members more conscious that he is a member of their group) and causing members to identify themselves more closely with the group. These ends are accomplished by:

- making the group more attractive to the worker: they find satisfaction of their needs for recognition, friendship, enjoyable work, etc.;
- maintaining open communication: employees can express their views and obtain information about the organization
- giving assistance: members can seek advice on personal problems as well as their work; and
- acting as a buffer between the group and management: he speaks up for his men and explains the reasons for management's decisions.

Such actions both strengthen group cohesiveness and solidarity and affirm the supervisor's leadership position in the group.

DEFINING MORALE

This brings us back to a point mentioned earlier. We had said that employee-centered supervisors contribute to high morale as well as to high production. But how can we explain units which have low morale and high productivity, or vice versa? Usually production and morale are considered separately, partly because they are measured against different criteria and partly because, in some instances, they seem to be independent of each other.

Some of this difficulty may stem from confusion over definitions of morale. Morale has been defined as, or measured by, absences from work, satisfaction with job or company, dissension among members of work groups, productivity, apathy or lack of interest, readiness to help others, and a general aura of happiness as rated by observers. Some of these criteria of morale are not subject to the influence of the supervisor, and some of them are not clearly related to productivity. Definitions like these invite findings of low morale coupled with high production.

Both productivity and morale can be influenced by environmental factors not under the control of group members or supervisors. Such things as plant layout, organizational structure and goals, lighting, ventilation, communications, and management planning may have an adverse or desirable effect.

We might resolve the dilemma by defining morale on the basis of our understanding of the supervisor as leader of a group; morale is the degree of satisfaction of group members with their leadership. In this light, the supervisor's employee-centered activities bear a clear relation to morale. His efforts to increase employee identification with the group and to strengthen his leadership lead to greater satisfaction with that leadership. By increasing group cohesiveness and by demonstrating that his influence and power can aid the group, he is able to enhance his leadership status and afford satisfaction to the group.

SUPERVISION, PRODUCTION, AND MORALE

There are factors within the organization itself which determine whether increased production is possible:

- Are production goals expressed in terms understandable to employees and are they realistic?
- Do supervisors responsible for production respect the agency mission and production goals?
- If employees do not know how to do the job well, does management provide a trainer—often the supervisor—who can teach efficient work methods?

There are other factors within the work group which determine whether increased production will be attained:

- Is leadership present which can bring about the desired level of production?
- Are production goals accepted by employees as reasonable and attainable?
- If group effort is involved, are members able to coordinate their efforts?

Research findings confirm the view that an employee-centered supervisor can achieve higher morale than a production-centered supervisor. Managers may well ask what is the relationship between this and production.

Supervision is production-oriented to the extent that it focuses attention on achieving organizational goals, and plans and devises methods for attaining them; it is employee-centered to the extent that it focuses attention on employee attitudes toward those goals, and plans and works toward maintenance of employee satisfaction.

High productivity and low morale result when a supervisor plans and organizes work efficiently but cannot achieve high membership satisfaction. Low production and high morale result when a supervisor, though keeping members satisfied with his leadership, either has not gained acceptance of organizational goals or does not have the technical competence to achieve them.

The relationship between supervision, morale, and productivity is an interdependent one, with the supervisor playing an integral role due to his ability to influence productivity and morale independently of each other.

A supervisor who can plan his work well has good technical knowledge, and who can install better production methods can raise production without necessarily increasing group satisfaction. On the other hand, a supervisor who can motivate his employees and keep them satisfied with his leadership can gain high production in spite of technical difficulties and environmental obstacles.

CLIMATE AND SUPERVISION

Climate, the intangible environment of an organization made up of attitudes, beliefs, and traditions, plays a large part in morale, productivity, and supervision. Usually when we speak of climate and its relationship to morale and productivity, we talk about the merits of *democratic* versus *authoritarian* climate. Employees seem to produce more and have higher morale in a democratic climate, whereas in an authoritarian climate, the reverse seems to be true or so the researchers tell us. We would do well to determine what these terms mean to supervision.

Perhaps most of our difficulty in understanding and applying these concepts comes from our emotional reactions to the words themselves. For example, authoritarian climate is usually painted as the very blackest kind of dictatorship. This is not surprising, because we are usually expected to believe that it is invariably bad. Conversely, democratic climate is drawn to make the driven snow look impure by comparison.

Now these descriptions are most probably true when we talk about our political processes, or town meetings, or freedom of speech. However, the same labels have been used by social scientists in other contexts and have also been applied to government and business organizations, without it, it seems, any recognition that the meanings and their social values may have changed somewhat

For example, these labels were used in experiments conducted in an informal classroom setting using 11-year-old boys as subjects. The descriptive labels applied to the climate of the setting as well as the type of leadership practiced. When these labels were transferred to a management setting, it seems that many presumed that they principally meant the king of leadership rather than climate. We can see that there is a great difference between the experimental and management settings and that leadership practices for one might be inappropriate for the other.

It is doubtful that formal work organizations can be anything but authoritarian, in that goals are set by management and a hierarchy exists through which decisions and orders from the top are transmitted downward. Organizations are authoritarian by structure and need; direction and control are placed in the hands of a few in order to gain fast and efficient decision making. Now this does not mean to describe a dictatorship. It is merely the recognition of the fact that direction of organizational affairs comes from above. It should be noted that leadership in some natural groups is, in this sense, authoritarian.

Granting that formal organizations have this kind of authoritarian leadership, can there be a democratic climate? Certainly there can be, but we would want to define and delimit this term. A more realistic meaning of democratic climate in organizations is the use of permissive and participatory methods in management-employee relations. That is, a mutual exchange of information and explanation with the granting of individual freedom within certain restricted and defined limits. However, it is not our purpose to debate the merits of authoritarianism versus democracy. We recognize that within the small work group there is a need for freedom from constraint and an increase in participation in order to achieve organizational goals within the framework of the organizational movement.

Another aspect of climate is best expressed by this familiar, and true, saying: actions speak louder than words. Of particular concern to us is this effect of management climate on the behavior of supervisors, particularly in employee-centered activities.

There have been reports of disappointment with efforts to make supervisors ore employee-centered. Managers state that, since research has shown ways of improving human relations, supervisors should begin to practice these methods. Usually a training course in human relations is established; and supervisors are given this training. Managers then sit back and wait for the expected improvements, only to find that there are none.

If we wish to produce changes in the supervisor's behavior, the climate must be made appropriate and rewarding to the changed behavior. This means that top-level attitudes and behavior cannot deny or contradict the change we are attempting to effect. Basic changes in organizational behavior cannot be made with any permanence, unless we provide an environment that is receptive to the changes and rewards those persons who do change.

IMPROVING SUPERVISION

Anyone who has read this far might expect to find *A Dozen Rules for Dealing With Employees* or *29 Steps to Supervisory Success*. We will not provide such a list.

Simple rules suffer from their simplicity. They ignore the complexities of human behavior. Reliance upon rules may cause supervisors to concentrate on superficial aspects of their relations with employees. It may preclude genuine understanding.

The supervisor who relies on a list of rules tends to think of people in mechanistic terms. In a certain situation, he uses *Rule No. 3*. Employees are not treated as thinking and feeling persons, but rather as figures in a formula: Rule 3 applied to employee X = Production.

Employees usually recognize mechanical manipulation and become dissatisfied and resentful. They lose faith in, and respect for, their supervisor, and this may be reflected in lower morale and productivity.

We do not mean that supervisors must become social science experts if they wish to improve. Reports of current research indicate that there are two major parts of their job which can be strengthened through self-improvement: (1) Work planning, including technical skills, and (2) motivation of employees.

The most effective supervisors combine excellence in the administrative and technical aspects of their work with friendly and considerate personal relations with their employees.

CRITICAL PERSONAL RELATIONS

Later in this chapter we shall talk about administrative aspects of supervision, but first let us comment on *friendly and considerate personal relations*. We have discussed this subject throughout the preceding chapters, but we want to review some of the critical supervisory influences on personal relations.

Closeness of Supervision: The closeness of supervision has an important effect on productivity and morale. Mann and Dent found that supervisors of low-producing units supervise very closely, while high-producing supervisors exercise only general supervision. It was found that the low-producing supervisors:

- check on employees more frequently
- give more detailed and frequent instructions
- limit employee's freedom to do job in own way

Workers who felt less closely supervised reported that they were better satisfied with their jobs and the company. We should note that the manner or attitude of the supervisor has an important bearing on whether employees perceive supervision as being close or general.

These findings are another way of saying that supervision does not mean standing over the employee and telling him what to do and when and how to do it. The more effective supervisor tells his employees what is required, giving general instructions.

COMMUNICATION

Supervisors of high-production units consider communication as one of the most important aspects of their job. Effective communication is used by these supervisors to achieve better interpersonal relations and improved employee motivation. Low-production supervisors do not rate communications as highly important.

High-producing supervisors find that an important aid to more effective communication is listening. They are ready to listen to both personal problems or interests and questions about the work. This does not mean that they are *nosey* or meddle in their employees' personal lives, but rather that they show a willingness to listen, and do listen, if their employees wish to discuss problems.

These supervisors inform employees about forthcoming changes in work; they discuss agency policy with employees; and they make sure that each employee knows how well he is doing. What these supervisors do is use two-way communication effectively. Unless the supervisor freely imparts information, he will not receive information in return.

Attitudes and perception are frequently affected by communication or the lack of it. Research surveys reveal that many supervisors are not aware of their employees' attitudes, nor do they know what personal reactions their supervision arouses. Through frank discussion with employees, they have been surprised to discover employee beliefs about which they were ignorant. Discussion sometimes reveals that the supervisor and his employees have totally different impressions about the same event. The supervisor should be constantly on the alert for misconceptions about his words and deeds. He must remember that, although his actions are perfectly clear to himself, they may be, and frequently are, viewed differently by employees.

Failure to communicate information results in misconceptions and false assumptions. What you say and how you say it will strongly affect your employees' attitudes and perceptions. By giving them available information, you can prevent misconceptions; by discussion, you may be able to change attitudes; by questioning, you can discover what the perceptions and assumptions really are. And it need hardly be added that actions should conform very closely to words.

If we were to attempt to reduce the above discussion on communication to rules, we would have a long list which would be based on one cardinal principle: Don't make assumptions!

- Don't assume that your employees know; tell them.
- Don't assume that you know how they feel; find out.
- Don't assume that they understand; clarify.

20 SUPERVISORY HINTS

1. Avoid inconsistency.
2. Always give employees a chance to explain their action before taking disciplinary action. Don't allow too much time for a "cooling off" period before disciplining an employee.
3. Be specific in your criticisms.
4. Delegate responsibility wisely.
5. Do not argue or lose your temper, and avoid being impatient.
6. Promote mutual respect and be fair, impartial, and open-minded.
7. Keep in mind that asking for employees' advice and input can be helpful in decision making.
8. If you make promises, keep them.
9. Always keep the feelings, abilities, dignity and motives of your staff in mind.
10. Remain loyal to your employees' interests.
11. Never criticize employees in front of others, or treat employees like children.
12. Admit mistakes. Don't place blame on your employees, or make excuses.
13. Be reasonable in your expectations, give complete instructions, and establish well-planned goals.
14. Be knowledgeable about office details and procedures, but avoid becoming bogged down in details.
15. Avoid supervising too closely or too loosely. Employees should also view you as an approachable supervisor.
16. Remember that employees' personal problems may affect job performance, but become involved only when appropriate.
17. Work to develop workers, and to instill a feeling of cooperation while working toward mutual goals.
18. Do not overpraise or underpraise, be properly appreciative.
19. Never ask an employee to discipline someone for you.
20. A complaint, even if unjustified, should be taken seriously.

NOTES

www.ingramcontent.com/pod-product-compliance
Lightning Source LLC
Chambersburg PA
CBHW081819300426
44116CB00014B/2422